A colour guide to familiar

WILD FLOWERS

Ferns and Grasses

D0625755

A colour guide to familiar
WILD FLOWERS
Ferns and Grasses

By Dr Bohumil Slavík

Illustrated by Vlastimil Choc

Translated by Daniela Coxon
Graphic design: Soňa Valoušková

This paperback edition published 1983 by
Octopus Books Limited
59 Grosvenor Street, London W 1

© 1973 Artia, Prague

ISBN 0 7064 1974 X

Printed in Czechoslovakia
3/10/01/51-10

CONTENTS

FOREWORD

The planet Earth abounds in immense beauty, to which the plant kingdom contributes a great deal. There are as many as 250,000 flowering plants and about the same number of ferns, mosses, fungi and their allies. Although there are places on the Earth where thousands of square kilometres are covered by only a few score of plant species, elsewhere the same number can be found in one square metre alone.

This book is not designed for specialists, but for a wide cross section of the reading public, and particularly for school children. It contains a collection of 64 colour plates of the most common plants. These can be found everywhere, by the roadside, in fields, meadows and woods, or close to house walls: nobody has to search very long for them. It is a pity that some people regard only exotic plants as beautiful and interesting, plants such as the orchids of tropical forests, the colourful lotuses of Indian rivers, the slender Mexican cacti or the tree ferns of eastern Asia. Yet the ordinary plants of woods, meadows and pastures have enough beauty of colour and form to captivate even the least observant among us, and please us with their pleasant, homely fragrance.

Probably because familiarity breeds neglect, there are people who every day, and, perhaps, throughout their lives, pass by such beauty without noticing it, as if their eyes were shut. Only when asked to name or describe them, do they become aware of their ignorance. This could be so simply remedied by taking the trouble to look closely at a meadow in summer or a woodland in spring with a pocket book of this kind to aid identification.

It is a sad fact that civilization continues with ever increasing determination to destroy the ties which through the ages have linked man and nature. Human progress is impressive, but the losses entailed are great. People of past ages had a greater knowledge of the various qualities of individual plants than today's generation. They knew from their own observation the seasonal development of plants, from spring through to winter, though they, perhaps, could not explain certain phenomena scientifically.

This book, then, presents a selection of plants and is accompanied by a brief summary of some natural processes. Its task will be accomplished if it encourages the reader to look more closely at our wild plants and to search for more detailed books to satisfy a growing interest.

Note: An asterisk* in the text denotes plants referred to in the pictorial section.

THE PLANT AND ITS ENVIRONMENT

A short walk in the countryside quickly reveals that the location of a plant is not an accidental or independent phenomenon, but that there is a certain interdependence between a particular plant species and its environment. Whilst the knotgrass (Polygonum aviculare*) springs up in gravel pathways and silvery green carpets of the silverweed (Potentilla anserina*) cover wayside or waste land, completely different species are found growing in a meadow, beside a stream, or in a wood. Similarly, the plants growing on sunny southern slopes will differ radically from those growing on northern ones, which may be only a few tens of metres distant. The difference is even more striking when the vegetation of the warm lowlands along the river Rhine is compared with that of the moorland areas by the North Sea, or with the vegetation of the high Alps.

Every plant more or less reflects the environmental conditions in which it grows, its habitat. The habitat comprises a complicated system of physical, chemical and biological interdependence, which is not constant. It is a complex of various ecological factors such as heat, cold, light, water, soil and wind. The change in any one factor is likely to modify the effect of the others.

The effectiveness of a plant's life cycle is dependent on the scale and strength of such individual ecological factors. Each plant species thrives best in certain conditions of light, heat and humidity. The functional limits of these ecological factors determine the characteristics of each species, subspecies, or variety of plant, and they can fluctuate between the minimum and maximum values of each factor. The plant stops growing outside these limits, and dies, when they are exceeded. The following chapters deal separately with the main factors which influence the growth of plants.

Heat or Cold?

All life processes can only take place in a certain temperature range. The temperature limits tolerable for plant life span a few tens of degrees centigrade. The sun's radiation is the only source of warmth, and only a small part of the radiation reaching the Earth's atmosphere is needed for the plant's energy requirement. In fact 43 % of the sun's radiation reaches the Earth's surface. Part of this 43% is reflected, radiated or lost elsewhere, and only the rest is absorbed by the plants and the soil. The top, microscopic layer of soil absorbs 30% to 50% of the radiation that penetrates it. The thermal differences between day and night, and between summer and winter, are greatest in this layer.

The quantity of absorbed and reflected warmth differs greatly in particular types of soil. The suitability of the growing media for a particular plant is obviously an important factor. Dark-coloured soils heat up more easily than the lighter ones; dry, sandy soils more than damp clay, or peat. The loose, crumbly soil of deciduous forests warms up very well as a result of high thermal conductivity, so that several warm, sunny days in spring are sufficient to stimulate the rhizomes and tubers of the wood anemone *(Anemone nemorosa*)* and lesser celandine *(Ranunculus ficaria*)*, lying dormant in the soil under the, as yet, leafless branches of trees.

How quickly the land warms up in spring is not simply dependent upon climatic conditions, or the type of soil, but also on the topography of the area, on its type of vegetation and, of course, on its geographical location.

The differences between the vegetation of northern and southern slopes should be common knowledge. (Fig. 1.) In exactly the same climatic and soil conditions completely different communities of plants arise, depending on the angle of the slope and on its aspect. Whilst drought-tolerant and

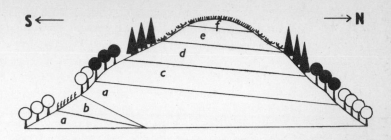

Fig. 1. Diagram showing influence of the altitude and the orientation of slopes on the distribution of vegetation: a — oak forests, b — warmth-loving grass formations on a secondary, deforested southern slope, c — beech forests, d — fir forests, e — dwarf pine forests, f — high-mountain meadows.

warmth-demanding plants grow on southern inclines, northern ones are populated by cool, moisture-loving species. The influence of the terrain (Fig. 2.) is particularly noticeable in deep gorges, where alpine plants can exist, even in low-lying positions, whilst warmth-demanding species thrive high above on the steep slopes. Different plants start to grow at different

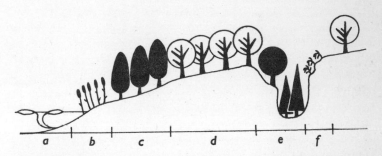

Fig. 2. Diagram showing how topographical features influence plant distribution:

a — aquatic plants, b — river bank reeds, c — woodland with willow trees and poplars, d — oak and hornbeam forests of hilly regions, e — deeply cut gorge with mountain spruce, fir and beech forest (inversion of degrees). f – rock vegetation.

temperatures. On a southern slope, with its snow cover melting at the end of winter, one can witness a beautiful sight. The blossoms of crocuses *(Crocus)*, snowdrops *(Galanthus)*, snowflakes *(Leucojum)* and other plants make their way towards the sun through the crystal beauty of the glittering ice. Soon after the snow has disappeared completely, meadows and grassy slopes burst into profusion of bright colours with anemones *(Anemone*)*, cowslip *(Primula veris*)*, kingcups *(Caltha palustris*)*, buttercups *(Ranunculus*)*, lady's smock *(Cardamine pratensis*)*, common violet *(Viola riviniana*)* and modest daisies *(Bellis perennis)*. These are all perennial plants, which store away in their underground organs (i.e. tubers, rhizomes or bulbs) the necessary nourishment for rapid growth, once conditions are suitable.

Germination also takes place only at a certain temperature. Whilst rye, fat hen *(Chenopodium album*)* or field poppy *(Papaver rhoeas*)* germinate at 1—2°C, maize needs 8—10°C, and melon and cucumber require temperatures as high as 14°C. The high germinating temperatures of melon and cucumber reflect the tropical and sub-tropical origin of these plants. There are also species whose seeds require a period at low temperatures, in some cases below 0°C, if they are to germinate at all.

The area of natural distribution of many plants roughly corresponds with certain climatic conditions, especially in terms of warmth and rainfall. However, macroclimatic data (i.e. the weather data for a large part of the Earth's surface) indicate only an approximate interdependence. The microclimate, the weather conditions of very small areas, such as a wood, a gorge or a sunny cliff, are more important. It is, unfortunately, very difficult to measure microclimatic values, and to draw general conclusions from them. In the following chapters, however, it will be shown that warmth is not the only essential factor in the life of plants.

No Life Without Water

The body of a living plant contains 50% to 98% water. Even seemingly dry seeds hold at least 8% to 15% water. The plant receives almost all its water from the soil. The roots act as a pumping device, and the root-hairs, which are tiny filamentous outgrowths near the tips of the rootlets, are the most active in this absorption process. The water travels from cell to cell, then enters the capillary system, which is often as much as several tens of metres in length. This water contains dissolved mineral salts, from which the plant builds up its body. In this respect it is hard to believe that only 0.2% of the total intake of water is directly involved in the body-building process. Of the remaining 99.8% a small amount maintains the plant's rigidity or turgor, which is the normal state of water tension in living cells; when the turgor decreases, the plant wilts. But by far the greatest part of the water simply evaporates into the air. In the temperate zone, a plant needs, on the average, 200 to 500 g of water with dissolved nutriments to produce 1 g of solid tissue. In dry regions, the amount is even higher.

The loss of water-vapour from plants is called transpiration. It takes place chiefly through small pores, known as stomata, on the green parts of plants, especially on leaves. The remaining part of the epidermis is capable of a slight transpiration, as long as it is not covered by an excessive layer of wax. The intensity of transpiration depends on the temperature of the air, on the water supply of the soil, on the condition of the stomata, and on the strength of the wind.

Transpiration can influence above all the climate of large woodland areas. In such regions, plants emit into the atmosphere an enormous volume of water-vapour. An area of 1 hectare (0.3861 of a square mile) of pine forest releases in summer 3 to 9.5 hectolitres of water per day; and the amount lost in deciduous forests is substantially higher. Each species of tree has a different transpiration rate; a fir tree has the lowest transpiration, the larch and the lime are in the middle category, and the poplar and alder are the most profuse.

Guttation is a specific way by which plants excrete water in the form of small drops. The droplets are discharged by water-excreting glands at the edges and tips of leaves. It is quite a common phenomenon in the vegetation of tropical forests, but it also occurs in cooler climates. In the morning after a warm summer night, when the air is saturated with water-vapour, water droplets reminiscent of dew glitter at the leaf edges of the lady's mantle *(Alchemilla mollis)*, the wild strawberry *(Fragaria vesca)* or on the tips of leaves of young corn.

Some aquatic plants can live without roots, but the majority of plants have a well-developed root system, which attaches the plant to the soil, and sometimes acts as food storage. But, above all, it ensures the system the supply of vital minerals dissolved in the water. To absorb these solutions, the plant has to overcome Earth's gravity and the forces which bind the water to the particles of soil. The absorbing power of the roots must be greater than the force binding the water to the soil. It fluctuates between 5 to 20 atmospheres with the majority of plants, and, in some desert plants it exceeds even 100 atmospheres in exceptional cases. (By way of illustration, the pressure in a car's motor, developed after the ignition of the compressed mixture, equals about 40—50 atmospheres.) By comparison the speed of the water flow in the stem is quite negligible, on the average 20 to 30 centimetres per hour, a distance which the blood in the veins of animals covers in less than a second.

The roots of individual species reach various depths. The majority of roots grow through the top layer of the soil to a maximum depth of 1.5 to 2 metres. However, many trees, and other plants, send roots much deeper. In some cases roots have been found at a depth of 15 to 18 metres. The greater the area of roots, especially the surface area of root hairs, the better is the contact with the water in the soil, and with the mineral solutions. The total length of all the roots, including the root hairs, is often considerable. For example, the fibrous roots of couch grass *(Agropyron cristatum)* grow to a depth of 2 metres, but their total length, including the root hairs, has been calculated at over 500 kilometres, and the total root length of the meadow grass *(Poa pratensis)* at about 74 kilometres. The total number of root hairs of such plants, which are just under 1 millimetre long, can be as much as several millions.

Rain, snow, dew and mist are the most important primary sources of water for all plants. The quantity of this precipitation, and its distribution over the year is of crucial importance in terms of the density of vegetation on the Earth's surface. In Europe rainfall decreases from west to east in accordance with the gradual change of the oceanic climate into the continental one. Rainfall, similarly, increases with the rise above sea level.

Plants can be divided into hydrophytes, hygrophytes, mesophytes and xerophytes according to their water needs. In addition, between these groups there are a number of intermediate categories.

Hydrophytes are completely dependent upon aquatic environment. They live either submerged in water, such as the Canadian pondweed *(Elodea canadensis)*, or their leaves float on the water surface, such as those of the water-lily *(Nymphaea)*. They are well equipped for such life.

Hygrophytes, moisture-loving plants, live in constantly wet or moist soil and are susceptible to drought conditions. Helophytes occur in all climatic conditions provided the soil is moist enough; particularly in water meadows, alongside streams and in marshes, where such plants as the marsh marigold *(Caltha palustris*)*, the lesser celandine *(Ranunculus ficària*)* and the lady's smock *(Cardamine pratensis*)* thrive. These plants usually have thin or somewhat fleshy leaves and, when picked, they fade quickly in the dry air. Mesophytes come between hygrophytes and xerophytes, and they form most of the European flora.

Xerophytes are adapted to live in dry conditions. They are able to stand up to prolonged drought conditions and low air humidity. They include succulents, plants which have fleshy leaves or stems (e.g. stonecrop [*Sedum**], houseleek [*Sempervivum*], cacti) and sclerophytes, plants with tough, often rolled or folded leaves, and a protective layer of wax or hairs on the epidermis, with the stomata concealed in pits within the epidermis (some drought resistant grasses, such as the fescues [*Festuca*]). Nevertheless, the dependence of plants on water is not the only criterion for classification.

The Miraculous Power of the Sun

Every year, about 20 cubic kilometres of vegetation are formed on the land surface of the world. This amount would form 20 thousand millions of cubes, each with a side 1 metre long. In contrast, the annual increase of plant life in the oceans is almost four times greater. The majority of this is formed by green plants, which are the primary producers of organic matter. Basically simple sources are needed for such production; they include chlorophyll, the green photosynthetic colouring matter, ordinary water and carbon dioxide. After that, the sun starts its work and the wheels of a countless number of miniature mills are set in motion. Thus begins the complicated process of photosynthesis; a photosynthetic assimilation, which is perhaps the most important process on the surface of this planet, since all life depends on it. Man has long been trying to copy it, but, as yet, without major success.

On its way through the atmosphere the sun's radiation loses much of its strength. This is caused by its dispersion and absorption by particles of the air, drops of water, dust and smoke. Only a percentage of direct radiation reaches the surface of the Earth, the rest is dispersed. The visible part of the spectrum is the most important for plants, although the ultra-violet radiation is also of some importance. It can, for instance, influence the growth of alpine species. The violet and red rays are the most important for the photosynthetic process.

Most people are, no doubt, aware of the importance of radiation, not only in terms of photosynthesis, but also for the production of chlorophyll itself. If not, it is sufficient to think of the yellowish white, lank potato stalks, which can be found in dark cellars in springtime, or of the yellowing of grass under a stone left lying on a lawn for several weeks. In such cases, plants grow excessively to reach the light as quickly as possible. If they succeed, they turn green and continue to flourish. The same happens with seeds that germinate deep down in the soil or are covered by a thick layer of compost. Quick growth and excessive lengthening of the cell structure is caused by a specific growth substance, which is only produced in quantity in the absence of light. Its existence can also be detected in other situations. Suppose a grass culm (stem) is flattened by the wind and is resting on the surface of the soil. Its underside is largely overshadowed and therefore the growth element is activated. Cells capable of renewed growth are found in the stem node; here they start to multiply with the result that the culm straightens into an upright position.

Some plants turn their blossoms to the sun as it travels through the sky during the day. Most striking of all is the movement of the sunflower, but similar behaviour is characteristic of a number of other plants, often members of the family *Compositae**, and also, for instance, of the wood anemone *(Anemone nemorosa*)*, if they grow in open spaces. Many plants turn their leaves, or other organs, towards the sun in order to maximize the use of the radiation. And some plants, mainly from hot dry areas, in order to prevent excessive overheating, turn their leaves edgeways up or hang them vertically down so that the sun rays only strike them obliquely. A good example can be seen in the prickly lettuce or compass plant *(Lactuca serriola)* often quite common by the wayside. The stem leaves are held vertically in the north-south plane and can be reliably used as a compass. Nature also provides timekeepers in several colours. Although they are not exact and vary with temperature and the time of year, they give rough estimates of time on a sunny day. Periodic observation of the closing and opening of some blossoms can prove interesting. The flower heads of the common dandelion *(Taraxacum officinale*)* and meadow buttercup *(Ranunculus acris*)* open between 6 and 7 a.m.; the blossoms of the mouse-ear hawkweed *(Hieracium pilosella*)*

and of the field bindweed *(Convolvulus arvensis*)* between 7 and 8 a.m., and those of the wood anemone *(Anemone nemorosa*)* and noble liverleaf *(Hepatica nobilis*)* as late as 9 and 10 a.m. In the afternoon blossoms start to close. The mouse-ear hawkweed as early as 1 to 2 p.m., the common dandelion between 2 and 3 p.m., the scarlet pimpernel *(Anagallis arvensis*)* between 3 and 4 p.m. and the dog rose *(Rosa canina)* as late as 8 or 9 p.m. But there are also plants that expand their blossoms more widely in the evening, as for instance the evening primrose *(Oenothera)*. Their fragrance attracts moths, which then pollinate them. However, it is impossible to provide a comprehensive survey of plant species with exact time data about their blooms, which would be valid everywhere under all conditions.

The dependence of plants on light is also apparent during the germination of their seed. Some seeds germinate only in the light, such as the mistletoe *(Viscum album)*, meadow grass *(Poa pratensis*)* and purple loosestrife *(Lythrum salicaria)*; others germinate only in the darkness at a certain depth under the soil surface (some members of the family *Chenopodiaceae**). Most plants, however, are quite indifferent in this respect and would germinate both in darkness or in light.

Mature plants also vary in their light requirements. Some need a high light intensity and are called sun-loving plants, or heliophytes. They grow on sunny rocks, on grassy slopes, on open wasteland and by the roadside, as for instance the wallpepper *(Sedum acre*)* and common thyme *(Thymus)*. They would not grow well in the shade of woods. As opposed to this, other species thrive there and are called shade-loving plants, or sciophytes.

Examples of these species are the common wood-sorrel *(Oxalis acetosella*)*, the common violet *(Viola riviniana*)* and the sweet woodruff *(Galium (Asperula) odoratum)*.

Interesting facts about the light requirements of plants can be observed in the forest. Plants grow here in several layers, one above the other. The largest amount of light is obviously absorbed by the top tree layer, but it must not be assumed that all trees have the same light needs. The commonest trees can be ranged into a group, at one end of which would be the shade-tolerant trees, which commonly grow beneath larger trees or in shady gorges and on northward slopes. This list might be graded as follows: Larch, birch, pine, common oak, ash, maple, lime, hornbeam, spruce, beech, fir and yew.

Further observation of forest vegetation will reveal other facts. The tops of trees, as already stated, absorb a considerable amount of light, and more is absorbed by developed shrubs. Only a negligible percentage of the total amount of light which falls on the tree tops reaches underlying plant growth. Sometimes it is so low (about 1%) that none of the green, vascular plants can survive. Similarly interesting conditions develop in some deciduous woods (Fig. 3.) In spring, before the trees start producing their leaves, plenty of light reaches the surface of the soil. Therefore, plants which require light spring up and start flowering, for instance wood anemone *(Anemone nemorosa)* and lesser celandine. However, as soon as the trees have a fully developed leaf cover the vegetation changes beyond recognition. It becomes dominated by the shade-loving species, which are content with 2% to 15% of the total amount of light. But, even the quality of such light cannot be compared with the direct light above the tree tops. Some colours are strongly filtered away by the tree leaves, so that the shade beneath them has a greenish or reddish shade (chlorophyll is bright green in transmitted light and red in reflected light).

Sometimes trees grow so densely that they envelop the plant life, which consequently receives less than the minimum amount of light. In such cases, if plants do not disappear completely, they survive in a vegetative state without forming any blossoms. If the trees are cut down, the nature of the undergrowth can change rapidly. The shade-loving species tend to be replaced by the typical light-demanding vegetation of the clearings, such as the rosebay willowherb *(Epilobium angustifolium*)* or the raspberry *(Rubus idaeus)*.

Each species, then, lives within certain light limits, expressed as a fraction of total light. In central European conditions the bilberry *(Vaccinium myrtillus)* can stand all degrees of light

Fig. 3. Simplifiod diagram showing the effect of direct radiation from the sun on a deciduous forest: A — in spring (a considerable intensity of light close to the ground, which heats up the soil and produces a rich ground flora), B — in summer (a decrease of the sun's energy, caused by the foliage of the tops of trees and leading to prevalence of shade-loving plants), a_1 — absorption of the sun's energy in the atmosphere, a_2 — reflection of the radiation in the atmosphere and the development of dispersed radiation, b_1 — absorption by vegetation (leaves), b_2 — reflection by vegetation, c_1 — absorption by the soil, c_2 — reflection by the soil.

from full strength down to 1/50 of it; other forest plants can survive in levels as low as 1/90 of total light. Again, different data would apply in southern regions and in the far north, where the light intensity, the proportion of direct and dispersed light, and the length of daylight is different. Some central European woodland species can be found in the tundra region of northern Europe in open sunny places, just as the species inhabiting the sunny slopes of central Europe can be found hidden in the shade of the mountainous forests of southern Europe.

The Nutritional Value of the Soil

The process of production of complicated organic matter from carbon dioxide and water has already been mentioned Nevertheless, the plant is not entirely formed from elements which derive from carbon dioxide and water (i.e. carbon, oxygen and water). Many other chemicals make up its composition; in some plants this number may exceed 50. These elements are not of equal importance. Some are vital for the majority of plants, others are important only for some species, while some elements are, we believe, unnecessary for plant life. The most important are nitrogen, phosphorus, potassium, calcium, magnesium, iron and sulphur. Some plants also contain copper, zinc, boron, arsenic and selenium, and, in certain individual cases, even chromium, vanadium, silver and other, more precious, elements have been detected. A higher content of silicon is found in the horsetail (Equisetum*), members of the Cyperaceae and Boraginaceae* families. A higher percentage of sulphur occurs in the cabbage family, a larger amount of sodium and potassium in many salt-loving plants, whilst aluminium is found in the clubmosses (Lycopodium) and selenium in some species of milk-vetch (Astragalus). Where do the plants acquire all these elements? By far the chief source is the soil. The soil is not a constant formation. It develops through the erosion of the basic rock and by the accumulation of organic matter. Many factors bring this about; initially the climate, and, then, vegetation, animals and sometimes man, along with various chemical and physical processes. For example, the type of basic rock influences the type and quality of the soil. Excellent, fertile soil for agricultural purposes develops from fine, glacial deposits. Also, some rocks are the basis of good soil, for example basalt, melamphyre and diabase, andesite and trachyte. Medium fertility soils develop from gneiss, mica-schist, phyllite, cretaceous marly limestone and marlite, whilst low fertility soils derive from limestone, dolomite and granite. Really poor soils evolve from serpentine, silicon sandstone and quartz. From the botanical point of view the soil is evaluated rather differently, the evaluation being based upon the richness of species. In this respect, the order of priority goes to soils originating from limestone, dolomite, serpentine, etc.

Erosion of the rocks produces fragmented material which provides the mineral basis for the future soil. True soil is then formed with the addition of organic matter, such as the remnants of dead plants and animals and with all the important micro-organisms such as algae and bacteria. All these processes take place simultaneously from the very beginning of the erosion. The bare rock is inhabited by bacteria, blue-green and green algae, which start to disintegrate its surface by exuding the products of their secretion, such as various acids. They also deposit the first dead organic matter and, with the help of rain, snow, sunshine, frost and wind, catch the first layer of dust. These fresh indentations and shallow hollows soon become the home of lichens and mosses, and later of vascular plants, including trees. Such rock-inhabiting plants inaugurate the continuous sequence of plant life, terminated by the typical plants which inhabit a fully formed soil layer.

One of the basic characteristics of the soil is its acidity or alkalinity; and this is related to the hydrogen ion concentration present in the soil. The degree of acidity and alkalinity is expressed on a numerical scale known as pH. Neutral soils measure 6.5—7 pH and alkaline soils are pH 7 and above. Really acid soils are pH 5 and below. The acidity of the soil is largely dependent on the chemical composition of the basic rock, on the humus content, and on the rainfall and climatic conditions. Vegetation is of secondary importance in terms of such chemical composition. Nevertheless, a spruce forest will produce an acid top soil; bilberry *(Vaccinium myrtillus)*, cowberry *(V. vitis-idaea)*, heather *(Calluna vulgaris*)* and some other plants also create a highly acid humus.

The content of calcium is also a determining factor in the quality of the substratum. By influencing the physical and chemical quality of the soil, it governs the character of the vegetation. It is usually present in the form of calcium carbonate. A number of plants, classified as calciphile, grow only in soils with a high calcium content. Such calcium-loving plants are the meadow oat *(Helictotrichon pratensis)*, whose small erect, oat-like flower spikes can be seen on dry grassy slopes, and a small fern, the wall-rue *(Asplenium ruta-muraria)*, which often grows in the plaster work of castle or church walls, and on fencing. On sunny, grassy slopes you may come across the blue-purple felwort *(Gentianella amarella)* and yellow-wort *(Blackstonia perfoliata)*. Even some field weeds may indicate calcareous soils, such as the annual mercury *(Mercurialis annua)*. Exceptionally, even some outstanding members of the orchid family, related to tropical orchids, such as the lady's slipper *(Cypripedium calceolus)*, the red helleborine *(Cephalanthera rubra)* or the deep reddish-violet dark-red-helleborine *(Epipactis atrorubens)* may be found growing in such soil. These all are protected in many countries.

There are many species of plants which, although preferring limestone soil, do not exclusively require it. To this category belong the well-known cowslip *(Primula veris*)*, white bryony *(Bryonia dioica)*, beech *(Fagus sylvatica)* and others. Also other common weed species often seem to prefer limestone soil, such as the wild charlock *(Sinapis arvensis*)*, as opposed to the similar wild radish *(Raphanus raphanistrum*)*.

An interesting phenomenon in terms of the distribution of plants, which is the subject of phytogeography, is the different location of two closely related species, one of which is dependent on limestone soil, and the other on siliceous, or acid, soil. This is especially noticeable in places where both types of soil occur in close proximity, especially in the mountains. A number of such species' pairs, one growing on a limestone, and the other on an acid, rock, can be found in the Alps. There are for example the hairy alpine rose *(Rhododendron hirsutum)* and the alpenrose *(R. ferrugineum)*, the stemless gentian *(Gentiana clusii)* and the broad-leaved gentian *(Gentiana kochiana)* and two species of primrose *(Primula auricula* and *P. villosa)*. The different requirements in terms of acid or alkaline soils are best illustrated by the *Rhododendron;* the optimal habitat of the alpine rose is soil with a pH of 5.5, whilst that of the hairy alpenrose is pH 7.3.

The vegetation of acid, siliceous soils, poor in nutriments, is monotonous and lacks the abundance of species which is characteristic of calcareous soils. Such vegetation is typical of the low-lying regions of central Europe. Here, the basic rock usually consists of granite, gneiss, mica-schist, porphyry, sandstone, etc. In the lowlands and the hills, such acid soils are generally overgrown with oak or pine forests, and in the mountains by spruce forests. When such forests are destroyed, they are replaced by poor quality pastures, acid meadows and fields, or other secondary vegetation, sometimes by heather moorland.

The usual indicators of acid soil are the heather *(Calluna vulgaris*)*, the bilberry *(Vaccinium myrtillus)*, the cowberry *(V. vitis-idaea)*, the sheep's sorrel *(Rumex acetosella*)*, etc. On entering a forest with an acid soil, one is attracted by the carpets of fine, silky, wavy hair-grass *(Deschampsia flexuosa)* and the tall growths of our largest fern, bracken *(Pteridium aquilinum*)*. In more open situations tufts of the sheep's fescue *(Festuca ovina)*, mouse-ear hawkweed *(Hieracium pilosella*)*, common cow-wheat *(Melampyrum pratense*)* and the light blue creeping common speedwell *(Veronica officinalis)* are found. Mountain slopes are often covered with large carpets of the small tufty mat grass *(Nardus stricta)*, whilst the siliceous soils of grassy slopes are revealed by the presence of the sweet vernal grass *(Anthoxanthum odoratum*)* or the sweeps' brush *(Luzula campestris*)*. The weeds of acid fields include the annual knawel *(Scleranthus annuus)*, wild radish *(Raphanus raphanistrum*)* and wild pansy *(Viola tricolor)*.

The vegetation can also be helpful in indicating the occurrence of certain minerals, even though they might be covered by a layer of soil. So far, the indicators of a wide group of lime and siliceous minerals have been mentioned, but there are also plants which direct attention to the presence of a specific mineral or element in the soil. Well known are the plants that indicate the presence of serpentine, a mineral with a high content of magnesium, enriched with the heavy metals, chrome and nickel. Similarly, other plant species indicate a deposit of copper, zinc or lead. They are most important in undeveloped areas, where there has been relatively little ore extraction, but they can be also found, to a small extent, in several parts of Europe on the spoil heaps of ore mines. For example in the Harz mountains, in soil with a high content of copper, the spring sandwort *(Minuartia verna* subsp. *hercynica)* grows, whilst a high concentration of zinc in the Rhine valley is indicated by special forms of the pansy *(Viola calaminaria)* and the pennycress *(Thlaspi calaminare)*; the existence of these "ore" plants has even revealed new deposits of zinc.

Halophytes form an important group of plants which grow in the soils of both coastal and inland regions with a high concentration of salts, especially of sulphates and chlorides. Salty soil has a highly alkaline reaction. Salt-tolerant plants, in contrast to other vegetation, can stand a high concentration of sulphates and chlorides in their cell structure, and are also able to regulate it in order to prevent damaging concentrations building up. The halophytic group consists mainly of the members of the *Chenopodiceae*, *Plumbaginaceae* and *Amarantaceae* families.

Several plants grow predominantly in soils with a high nitrogen content. These plants are commonly known and easily seen; they can be found in close proximity to human dwellings, on village greens, near fences, in backyards, gardens, on compost heaps, in ditches and on wasteland. To them belong, for example, the common nettle *(Urtica dioica*)*, silverweed *(Potentilla anserina*)*, dwarf mallow *(Malva neglecta*)*, knotgrass *(Polygonum aviculare*)*, rye-grass *(Lolium perenne*)*, fat hen *(Chenopodium album*)*, and the strongly poisonous members of the *Solanaceae* family. In the mountains, near chalets and cattle enclosures, the strikingly large monk's rhubarb *(Rumex alpinus)*, which needs soil with a high content of nitrogenous salts, is often widespread. The growths of the monk's rhubarb survive long after the disappearance of chalets and cattle and thus indicate to us the history of such places. Other nitrogen indicators can be found growing in virgin, uncultivated soils such as river banks and, especially, in riverside forests, where yearly flooding enriches the soil with minerals and organic matter. Typical species of this kind of soil are the touch-me-not *(Impatiens noli-tangere)*, hedge garlic *(Alliaria officinalis)*, greater celandine *(Chelidonium majus)*, goosegrass *(Galium aparine)*, common nettle *(Urtica dioica*)*, herb bennet *(Geum urbanum)*, goutweed *(Aegopodium podagraria*)*, etc.

The Wind as Helper and Destroyer

The layer of air above the Earth's surface is in constant motion. The irregularity in the speed and direction of the wind varies according to the number of obstacles it encounters, and the general profile of the terrain. Even the slightest breeze can influence the character of vegetation; a strong gale can devastate many hectares of woods and change the whole character of a region in a very short space of time.

The wind is instrumental in scattering the spores, seeds or fruits of plants. It can carry spores and light seeds several hundred or even thousand kilometres. In this way, plants have been introduced to remote, ocean islands, to the steep peaks of high mountains and into desert wastes. But, at the same time, the wind enables the spores of plant diseases and weed seeds to penetrate gardens, fields and orchards.

The wind is also an important pollination agent. Almost one fifth of the vegetation living in our climatic conditions is pollinated by the wind. The list would include all coniferous and catkin trees, grasses and other plants, as for instance the common nettle *(Urtica dioica*)* and the fat hen *(Chenopodium album*)*. The flowers of these plants are variously modified for wind pollination. Because they do not need to attract insects, they are inconspicuous, often lacking sepals and petals, dull in colour and have neither scent nor nectar. The stamens of grasses have versatile anthers on long filaments and the hazel and poplar catkins swing lightly on long stalks. As there is only a very slight chance of a pollen grain falling on to the stigma of another flower, a lot of pollen is produced.

In some areas of the Earth's surface, the wind has been blowing predominantly in one direction for centuries. This happens in unprotected coastal regions, on windward mountain slopes and on mountain ridges and peaks high above the forest belt. Plants exposed to such winds acquire after some time characteristic shapes. An example of this phenomenon is the distinctive flag shape of a spruce, pine or sycamore growing at the seashore. Similarly, high mountain plants resist strong winds by forming tight and compact cushions, or dense, ball-shaped clusters. The wind also influences the physiology of plants. It blows away the water evaporated from leaf surface and thereby stimulates further transpiration to take place. Such mountain plants are often covered with woolly hairs to minimize water loss. Persistent, or strong wind, can also have a damaging effect, as it causes dehydration and, finally, the drying up of individual organs, and even of the whole plant. In addition, the wind can greatly influence the composition of the atmosphere, which in turn can have either a beneficial or an adverse effect on the photosynthetic process. The regulation of the amount of carbon dioxide in the air is of crucial importance in this respect.

PLANT DISPERSAL

If all the hundreds or thousands of seeds or fruits produced by a plant fell directly underneath it and began to germinate, what would be the consequences? The soil, already partly exhausted by the mother plant, would not be able to feed even a small proportion of the germinating seeds, while the shade of the mother plant would inhibit the healthy growth of the seedlings. The water supply might, also, be insufficient. All this would mean this particular plant species would not spread any further, bare rocks would never be covered by vegetation, and vast spaces would remain without any life.

Nature, however, has prevented such a situation with surprising ingenuity. By one means or another, many of the seeds, fruits and other units of plant dispersal do get away from the mother plant, enough, at least, to multiply and spread the species. Sometimes this means only a few centimetres, but at other times even tiny seeds can travel hundreds of kilometres. The unit of dissemination does not always find suitable conditions for further development. Plants overcome this problem by the excessive production of spores and seeds, and so increase the probability of survival.

A closer analysis of the modes of dissemination of various types of fruits and seeds will reveal the way they travel and the adaptations that evolution has provided to achieve such mobility.

The wind is one of the most common agents of movement. The weight of many seeds, and of all spores, is negligible, and can be measured in thousandths or millionths of a gram. In some cases, the particles of atmosphere brought to the earth by rain are found to contain the spores of plants whose nearest known place of origin is several thousand kilometres off. Seed-producing plants with unusually light seeds include members of the *Orchidaceae, Ericaceae*, Gramineae** and other families.

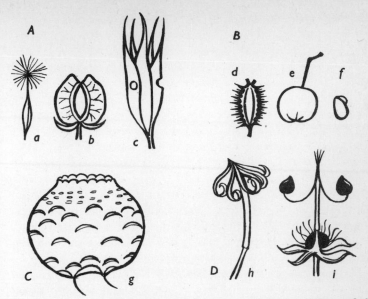

Fig. 4. Fruits and seeds distributed by: A — wind (a — achene of the dandelion, b— achene of the sorrel, c — capsule of the harebell), B — animals (d — double achene of the carrot, e — berry of the mistletoe, f — seed of the viola with a carnic outgrowths), C — water (g — capsule of the water lily), D — mother plant (h — capsule of the touch-me-not, i — beaked fruit of the meadow cranesbill).

A number of seeds and fruits are equipped with various kinds of appendages to make them buoyant in air. Most often this is a small tuft of soft hair, which serves as a parachute. It develops from the calyx on the achenes of the common dandelion *(Taraxacum officinale*)*, hawkweed *(Hieracium*)*, coltsfoot *(Tussilago farfara*)*, and various species of thistles *(Cirsium** and *Carduus)*. Often in June, you may find the air full of flying white "fluff" — the long-haired seeds of willows and poplars. One comes across the same phenomenon in summer in woodland clearings, when the seeds of the rosebay willow-herb *(Chamaenerion angustifolium*)* have ripened. In each case the outgrowth of hairs is direct from the seed coat.

The gliding motion of fruits and seeds of some trees makes a wonderful sight. Each fruit and seed is equipped with a membranous outgrowth which serves as a wing. The fruits of the maple and ash are equipped with rigid, well-developed wings, limes have persistent, enlarged bracts, whereas the achenes of elms and birches have semicircular or flange-like outgrowths. Other plants have relatively heavy seeds, without a flying attachment, and yet the wind is still an important factor in their dissemination. The capsules of the bellflowers *(Campanula*)* or of some poppies (the field poppy [*Papaver rhoeas**]) open at the top, so that the seeds are catapulted out when the wind flips the stalk. They are sometimes cast quite a distance from the parent plant.

Another large group of plants bears seeds and fruits which are distributed by animals. The range of devices the seeds and fruits employ, enabling such a means of dissemination, is very extensive, including hooks, spines (sometimes barbed) and other protrusions by which the seeds and fruits fix themselves to the hair and feathers of animals. They are characteristic of the fruits of wood avens *(Geum urbanum)*, bur marigold *(Bidens tripartita)* and wild carrot *(Daucus carota)*. In some cases, the whole plant is equipped with clinging hooks, such as the goosegrass *(Galium aparine)*. Birds can disseminate fruits and seeds in two ways; by picking them up, in the feathers on their bodies, or in the mud on their feet, and by actually feeding on berries and fruits. The seeds within pass through the digestive tract unharmed and are voided in their droppings. In this way the wild cherry *(Prunus avium)*, bilberry *(Vaccinium myrtillus)*, gooseberry *(Ribes grossularia)*, mountain ash *(Sorbus aucuparia)* and mistletoe *(Viscum album)* have been introduced to otherwise inaccessible places.

Another interesting group is the plants whose seeds are disseminated by the activity of ants. Their seeds are endowed with fleshy protrusions known as caruncles or arils, which are rich in fat or oil and beloved by ants. Seeds can be carried tens of metres along the tracks leading to an anthill. Some seeds are lost on the way, and ants eat the juicy parts of the rest in the anthill, later scattering the undamaged seeds in the adjacent neighbourhood. This is how some plants, such as the greater celandine *(Chelidonium majus)*, appear on high walls, or sprout from the hollow tree trunks of the weeping willow, high above the ground. These seeds with fleshy protrusions are produced by several species of woodland plants, for instance the common hepatica *(Hepatica nobilis*)*, lesser celandine *(Ranunculus ficaria*)*, cow-wheat *(Melampyrum*)*, woodrush *(Luzula*)*, fumewort *(Corydalis)* and lungwort *(Pulmonaria)*.

Not the least important agent in plant distribution is man. He is responsible for some of the variety of species found on ·wasteland, rubbish tips, in fields and by roadsides. Uncountable numbers of seeds have been transferred on the wheels of vehicles, on the fuselages of planes, or in packing cases with wool, cotton and other goods en route, far from their homeland, to distant destinations, often to other continents. Furthermore, newly-introduced species can often be found, especially near ports or container depots, in flour refineries and cotton factories, or on the wasteland of large cities.

The seeds of aquatic and waterside plants, i.e. water-lily *(Nymphaea)*, yellow water-lily *(Nuphar)*, yellow flag *(Iris pseudacorus)*, kingcup *(Caltha*)*, are able to float for a long time in the water surface. This is made possible by the air-filled spaces of their internal structure. Water is, similarly, a decisive factor in scattering the seeds of some terrestrial plants, but flowing surface water, which occurs especially after a heavy downpour, and not the water of rivers, lakes and ponds. In this way, the seeds of some species of the speedwell *(Veronica*)*, the knotgrass *(Polygonum*)* and the plantain *(Plantago*)* are carried away.

Perhaps the most interesting group of plants comprises those which disperse their seeds mechanically. Such plants catapult or eject their seeds into their surroundings. When the capsules of all species of touch-me-not (for example the yellow balsam [*Impatiens noli-tangere*], small balsam [*I. parviflora*] or the tall policeman's helmet [*I. glandulifera*]) are touched, they burst instantly, and the seeds travel to a distance of several metres from the mother plant. Some other plants which expel their ripe seeds in a similar way are the cranesbills *(Geranium*)*, wood sorrel *(Oxalis acetosella*)*, spurges *(Euphorbia*)*, violets *(Viola*)*, vetch *(Vicia)* and many others.

PLANT DISTRIBUTION

The various ways in which plants are distributed over the Earth's surface have been mentioned in the last chapter. Some movements are measured only in metres, whilst others travel long distances of several hundred kilometres. However, no species can develop successfully in every single one of the places to which their seeds or spores are brought by wind, water or by animals. Each species has specific, environmental requirements and if these are not present it will not germinate. If it does, it soon gives way to other stronger species, which are better suited to the particular conditions; or it dies for other reasons.

Each plant species, genus or family has its own limiting factors for growth. If these are not present it will not thrive. However, it would be unwise to state that all plants are not able to survive outside these limits. The extension of such boundaries, sometimes even over large areas, can be simply a question of time under normal conditions of development; or it can be the outcome of human intervention, which results in the artificial removal of restricting barriers. The limited surface occupied by a species is called its distribution area.

A few species, their number amounting only to a few dozen, are naturally widespread over the greater part of the Earth's surface and are described as cosmopolitan (cosmop. for short). Even these are not present everywhere. The majority of them are ferns or mosses, because of the relative ease by which their spores can be scattered. Of the plants listed in this book the most extensive fern of temperate forests, the bracken *(Pteridium aquilinum*)*, is a good example of this category. The majority of cosmopolitan higher plants are aquatic and marsh species, as the water and marsh environment has many constant and similar characteristics throughout the world. Water-fowl also contribute to this general feature, by carrying seeds on their feet and feathers on their journeys, which can stretch for many thousands of kilometres. A good example is the common reed *(Phragmites communis)*, which grows not only in European ponds, but also in the lakes of North and South America and in eastern Asia.

The third group of cosmops includes weeds that have been scattered all over the world by man. Only very adaptable plants, which can tolerate a wide range of environmental conditions, come into this category. One such plant is the annual meadow grass *(Poa annua*)*, which can be found in Nüremberg, and in London, in remote villages in northern Scandinavia and in the centre of Tokyo, on the banks of Canadian lakes and on isolated islands in the stormy seas close to the Antarctic.

The knotgrass *(Polygonum aviculare*)*, shepherd's purse *(Capsella bursa-pastoris*)* and ribwort plantain *(Plantago lanceolata*)* are similarly widespread over the Earth.

The complete antithesis of cosmops are plants which are restricted to a very small area, sometimes extending only over several square kilometres. They are called endemics, and are often the remnants of a once-thriving species in process of dying out. They constitute important rarities in the flora of their native land. *Jankaea heldreichii*, a European representative of the tropical *Gesneriaceae* family, does not grow anywhere else but on Mount Olympus, the home of the gods of Ancient Greece. Similarly the Slovak mezereon *(Daphne arbuscula)* grows only on the limestone cliffs of the Muran region in Slovakia, while *Saxifraga paradoxa* of the *Saxifragaceae* family is only found in several places in Carinthia and Styria. Species of endemics are still developing. For instance, in European mountain ranges, dozens of such species have evolved during the last thousand years. Some of these species are members of the hawkweed *(Hieracium)*, saxifrage *(Saxifraga)*, primrose *(Primula)* and the gentian *(Gentiana)* genera.

Some plants live in restricted areas, within which they are often common, or even abundant. In Europe, such species are represented by deciduous trees, the common and durmast oak *(Quercus robur, Q. petraea)* or the ash *(Fraxinus excelsior)*, and herbs like cow-wheat *(Melampyrum nemorosum)*, germander speedwell *(Veronica chamaedrys*)* or the common hepatica *(Hepatica nobilis*)*. Some other species grow scattered in small areas separated by similar terrain where they also should grow, but do not. This may indicate that the particular species, such as the Austrian ribseed *(Pleurospermum austriacum)*, is dying out, or declining, as a result of gradual climatic changes, or that it is giving way to a more vigorous species which is colonizing new areas, such as the alpine penny-cress *(Thlaspi alpestre)*.

The area inhabited by a particular species may often be enlarged by human activity. As some regions of North America have a very similar climate to that of Europe, it is not surprising that, after the discovery of America, the migration of North American plants to Europe, and vice versa, took place. This mutual exchange of species between continents has continued for almost half a millenium and, nowadays, in some cases it is difficult to decide whether a particular plant was originally introduced or not. Some species have, indeed, become so perfectly naturalized that they give the impression of being native.

The history of the introduction, naturalization and discovery of the majority of these species would fill hundreds of pages and provide a thrilling story. For example, the South American gallant soldier *(Galinsoga parviflora)* is today one of the most widespread weeds in fields and gardens. However, it began its journey across the European continent very modestly, originating at the beginning of the last century in the Botanical Garden in Berlin. Indeed, many such plants were grown originally in Botanical Gardens. The Siberian small-flowered balsam *(Impatiens parviflora)* spread over the walls of the Botanical Gardens in Geneva and Dresden in the 1830s, and, since then, it has succeeded in displacing the native European touch-me-not *(I. noli-tangere)* from long stretches of river banks. Similarly, the sweet flag *(Acorus calamus)*, nowadays abundant on the banks of lakes and quiet rivers, is not a European native. It was imported in the second half of the 16th century as a rarity from Constantinople to European Botanical Gardens. From these gardens, and mainly from the Viennese one, it

Fig. 5. Simplified phytogeographic division of Europe into floristic regions: a — arctic, b — boreal, c — atlantic, d — central European and east European, e — pontic, f — sub-Mediterranean, g — Mediterranean, h — Aral-Caspian, dotted — alpine.

started invading wild habitats. Other typical introduced species are the common Canadian fleabane *(Conyza canadensis)*, which was found growing wild in France in the first half of the 17th century and, subsequently, in England, Germany, Poland and other countries; and also the beggar-ticks *(Bidens frondosa)*, the Canadian pondweed *(Elodea canadensis)*, the upright yellow sorrel *(Oxalis europaea)*, the slender rush *(Juncus tenuis)* and the Buxbaum's speedwell *(Veronica persica)*. The majority of plants introduced into Europe come from North America or Asia, but African and Australasian species are only rarely represented because of the considerable differences in habitat.

Botanists have divided the Earth's flora into a complicated system of floristic regions, based on the differences and similarities within and between the regions, against the background of climate. Classification of the European flora is the major concern here, however. It has already been discussed by many authors, who often differ significantly, but the system of basic units usually remains constant. Fig. 5 gives a brief, simplified summary of this system.

The most northerly part of Europe is the home of the arctic plants of the tundra (the rock whitlow grass [*Draba norvegica*] and polar willow [*Salix polaris*]). The growing season here is very short, lasting only 2 to 3 months of each year. The low temperatures prevent the growth of trees. The development of the tree vegetation starts in the adjacent climatic zone, the wide belt of northern coniferous forests. Plant species characteristic of this zone are, therefore, qualified by the epithet boreal (northern). Some of them grow sporadically in central Europe, as for instance the twinflower *(Linnaea borealis)* or bearberry *(Arctostaphylos uva-ursi)*. Towards the north-eastern parts of central Europe the boreal species have become increasingly mixed up with another floristic element, namely the flora of central European deciduous forests. Apart from some deciduous trees (beech, oak, hornbeam, maple) this element also includes some herbs, such as the common hepatica *(Hepatica nobilis*)*, the cow-wheat *(Melampyrum nemorosum)* and the lily-of-the-valley *(Convallaria majalis)*.

The high degree of atmospheric humidity, and the associated abundant rainfall, occurring in a wide band of territory along the Atlantic from Portugal up to central Norway, are responsible for the development of the characteristic Atlantic flora. The oceanic climate with cool summers and mild winters evidently has no sharply defined border to the east, but instead gradually merges into a continental climate. In accordance with this gradual change, the true Atlantic flora slowly fades out (e.g. the cross-leaved heath [*Erica tetralix*] — fig. 6), and gives way to the sub-Atlantic species (heather [*Calluna vulgaris**]), which, in turn, disappears completely in eastern Europe. A similar process of gradual replacement can also be traced

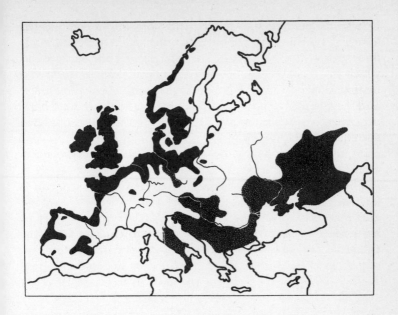

Fig. 6. Distribution of the cross-leaved heath *(Erica tetralix)* — black — and of the Illyrian buttercup *(Ranunculus illyricus)* — dotted.

in the opposite direction. In this case, Pontic species gradually come into the picture, such as the Illyrian buttercup *(Ranunculus illyricus)*, (fig. 6.) which thrives in the continental climate of the dry steppe regions in the south European part of the Soviet Union. These species also penetrate central Europe across the Hungarian plain to Moravia and central Bohemia, and many of them are still found in Thüringia, in the upper reaches of the River Rhine, and along the River Main. Central Europe is also penetrated by another floristic element from the south, namely the sub-Mediterranean zone. In contrast to Pontic species, which can stand quite low temperatures in winter, the sub-Mediterranean species prefer the warm, southerly slopes, where even the winter temperatures are higher than anywhere else. They can be represented here by the pubescent oak *(Quercus pubescens)* and the perennial lettuce *(Lactuca perennis)*. Finally, the distinctive Mediterranean flora grows in the zone adjacent to the Mediterranean Sea, which is characterized by strikingly dry summers with high temperatures, and rainfall mainly during the mild autumn and winter. Such species are the olive *(Olea europaea)* and the evergreen oak *(Quercus ilex)*. Besides these groups, we should also mention the specific floras of high mountain regions, especially those of the Alps and the Carpathians, which belong to alpine floristic element.

The contemporary state of European flora is a result of far-reaching climatic changes which took place in the glacial and postglacial periods. Nevertheless, without the pervasive influence of man, the vegetation, especially in the lowlands, would be radically different from its present state.

The colour plates are arranged roughly in seasonal sequence, according to the time when the plants depicted are in bloom, extending from early spring until autumn. The text which accompanies each plant species gives a brief description.

The Roman numerals relate to the months when the plant is in blossom and, in the case of the horsetail and ferns, to the time of the formation of spores. These numbers are followed by symbols which indicate the duration of life of a particular plant.

$\odot$ = annual
$\odot$ = biennial (or winter-annual)
$\mathsf{2\!\!\!\perp}$ = perennial

The average height of a plant is given in centimetres. The summary of the main features of a plant is followed by an indication of its approximate distribution:

Eu. = Europe
As. = Asia
Am. = America
Af. = Africa
Au. = Australia
N. Z. = New Zealand
ccsm. = cosmopolitan
N. = North
E. = East
W. = West

Coltsfoot

Tussilago farfara L.

The yellow heads of the coltsfoot burst into flower in the first warm, spring days at the edges of ditches, on banks, in quarries and in fields. They appear, on red, flushed scaly stems, well before the first leaves. As the flowers fade, the bold rounded leaves appear direct from the rootstock buds. The coltsfoot prefers damp, heavy, yet fertile soils, preferably containing lime. It can be a troublesome weed in fields as it spreads excessively by a complex system of long rootstocks (rhizomes) and also by quantities of seeds. The latter can start to germinate in less than 24 hours under ideal conditions of moisture and warmth. Luckily, their period of viability does not last longer than 2—3 months.

The coltsfoot has been one of the most important herbs used for medicinal purposes since ancient times. The physicians of Ancient Greece recommended the inhalation of the smoke from its roots, when burnt on cypress coal, as a cough remedy. Its leaves dried and mixed with tobacco were also smoked as a remedy for asthma. The leaves, it is claimed, speed up the healing of wounds and skin diseases, and were used as compresses for rheumatic pains.

III—IV; ♃ ; 5—15 cm when in bloom; 20—30 cm when fruit is developed. *Rhizome:* Creeping. *Stems:* Scaly with solitary flower heads. *Leaves:* After flowering, rounded, cordate, shallowly lobed, with white-felted undersides. *Seeds:* Achenes with a parachute of long hairs. Eu., As., N. Af.; introduced in N. Am.

1 — achene

1

Common Hepatica

Hepatica nobilis MILL.
(Syn. *Anemone hepatica* L.)

The buttercup
family
Ranunculaceae

The blue flowers of the common hepatica are a characteristic sign of spring. As soon as the soil warms up a little, the pale purple-blue flowers start to emerge from the rootstocks hidden beneath the leaves, and soon attract early insects. In the main, they are found in oak, beech and oak-hornbeam forests, but grow also in large numbers on bushy slopes under hazel trees. The common hepatica likes lime soils, and so does not grow everywhere in Europe. It does not occur in England, in the Netherlands and in Greece, and, even in some countries where it grows, there are regions where it is rare or completely absent. As a result, it is protected in Germany and Switzerland.

The blossoms of the common hepatica remain open for about a week, closing and bending over at night, and during rain. The floral parts are thus protected against the effects of the cold night air, the dew and the rain. The ripe achene has an oily swelling at its base, which is a great delicacy for ants. Such insects are, therefore, its main distributors. This type of distribution is very slow, so that the plant advances only 5—10 metres in a year. The expansion is sometimes stopped by obstacles, for example wide,˙ or fast, rivers which prove insurmountable for the ants.

III—V; ♃;
5—15 cm.
Rhizome:
Creeping.
Leaves: Petiolate,
trilobate.
Flowers:
3 small, ovate,
entire bracts with
entire margins
enfold the blossom
in bud, acting as
a calyx.
Petals:
6—9, blue purple.
Stamens and pistils:
Many.
Achenes:
Hairy with
a short beak.
Eu.

1 — fruits enclosed
by the 3
persistent floral
bracts

1

Wood Anemone

Anemone nemorosa L.

The buttercup family
Ranunculaceae

The wood anemone is one of the commonest spring plants, blooming soon after the last snow, or severe frost, has melted away. The flowering buds appear on the yellow-brown rootstocks in the soil as early as the autumn of the preceding year. In spring, they force their way through to the surface after several warm days, and flood the light, deciduous woods, the river banks, and mountain slopes with their white blossoms.

Early in spring, there are only a few insects about to pollinate the flowers. Moreover, the blossoms of the wood anemone have little attraction for insects as they give only pollen, not nectar, so that seeds develop only from a few flowers. If some of them ripen, they often fall among dry leaves, where they cannot germinate. What is the reason then for the wood anemone forming large growths in so many places? This is due to its creeping rootstock, which grows and branches out continuously at one end, while dying away at the other. Thus, it persistently spreads a few centimetres to new areas every year. The wood anemone contains a slightly poisonous substance called protoanemonine.

III—V; ♃; 10—20 cm.
Rhizome: Slender, creeping.
Leaves: Usually one petiolate radical leaf, palmately divided into 3-toothed segments; three 3-lobed, whorled stem-leaves.
Flowers: With 6 to 8 white or pink-tinged petals, glabrous on the outside.
Achenes: Slightly hairy with a curved beak. Eu.

1 — fruit

1

Field Woodrush or Sweep's Brush

Luzula campestris LAM. et DC.

The rush family
Juncaceae

The field woodrush, reminiscent of grasses, flowers on grassy, lowland slopes, and mountain sides, in early spring. It has no value as a fodder plant, and so, for purposes of husbandry it is classified as a meadow weed.

The field woodrush as a species shows wide variety. It is sometimes merged with the closely related species, the many-headed woodrush (*L. multiflora* [Retz.] Lej.). The field woodrush forms loose tufts from a stoloniferous rootstock; the flowering stems are 5—15 cm tall, the anthers 2—6 times longer than the filaments; it flowers earlier than the many-headed woodrush, which grows in dense tufts without stolons. Its stem is 20—50 cm tall and the anthers are only a little longer than the filaments. The former grows on well-drained, sunny, grassy slopes, close to roads and on banks; the latter inhabits damp meadows, light woods, clearings, moorlands and grasslands in the mountains.

III—V; $2\!\!\downarrow$;
5—50 cm.
Rhizome:
Creeping.
Stems: Erect.
Leaves: Ciliate,
2—5 mm broad.
Inflorescence:
Many-flowered;
perianth
segments
lanceolate, brown,
with membranous
margins.
Fruit:
Oval capsule.
Almost cosm.

1 — flower

1

Field Horsetail

Equisetum arvense L.

The field horsetail can be a very annoying weed in gardens and fields, as its rootstocks reach a length of 7 metres and grow to a depth of 2 metres. The rootstock produces two types of stems; in spring, the fertile, yellowish stem, which takes in nourishment. The spring stems produce a large number of spores which, when highly magnified, reveal two spiral bands, attached at their centres, forming 4 arms. These bands react to dampness by curling up, and only stretch out again when the weather is dry. The outstretched arms or bands of each spore have curled tips, creating the appearance of a four pronged grapple. Adjacent spores become intertwined and are dispersed by the wind in groups. This is an essential advantage as the spores develop into separate-sexed bodies (prothalli). Being clustered together it is more likely that fertilization will take place.

The sterile stems contain 7%—10% of silicic oxide and so are rough, lowering the quality of the green fodder and the hay with which it is mixed. They were used for cleaning metal utensils and for polishing wood and horn. The herbage was boiled and the resulting liquid, which has diuretic properties, was also used externally for healing ulcerous wounds. A high content of the herbage in fodder can cause paralysis, especially among horses.

III—V; ♃;
10—40 cm.
Rhizome:
Segmented.
Spring stems:
Yellowish or brownish with 8—12 toothed sheaths.
Sporangia:
In a terminal cone.
Sporangiophores:
Peltate.
Summer stems:
Green, with whorled leaves. Northern hemisphere.

1 — spring stem with rhizome,
2 — summer stem,
3 — shield-like sporangiophore bearing sporangia (which contain the minute spores)

Lesser Celandine or Pilewort
Ranunculus ficaria L.

The buttercup
family
Ranunculaceae

The glossy, bright yellow flowers and shiny leaves of this variable plant have given it many folk names. The lesser celandine often forms dense colonies in damp places in woods, riverside forests, on the bushy banks of streams, in damp meadows, in orchards, parks and gardens. It indicates the presence of a fertile, humus-rich soil both in the lowlands and the mountains. In summer, all the parts above ground die off and only the clusters of elongated fig-shaped root tubers remain in the soil ready for the following spring's display. Sometimes tiny bulbils develop in the axils of the basal or stem leaves, but the plants which develop from them take two years or more to reach flowering size.

Young spring plants contain a quantity of vitamin C and therefore can be used in the preparation of a spring salad. When young, lesser celandine is not dangerous, but later it develops a bitter taste and is poisonous. This is caused by the presence of the substance protoanemonine, found in several members of the buttercup family. Some forms of lesser celandine are partially sterile and may not produce seeds.

III—V; 2|;
5—20 cm.
Roots:
Fibrous with root tubers.
Stems:
Ascending.
Leaves:
Stalked, sparsely crenate or shallowly lobed and shiny.
Flowers: On separate stalks with 4—5 sepals and 8—12 bright yellow petals.
Achenes:
Spherical, keeled and more or less minutely downy.
Eu.

Shepherd's Purse

Capsella bursa-pastoris (L.) MED.

The cabbage
family
Cruciferae

The shepherd's purse is one of the commonest weeds, growing on cultivated soils as well as on wasteland all over the temperate world. It is very hardy and sometimes it flowers in the depth of winter. It is not easy to eradicate, as one well-developed plant can produce as many as 50,000 seeds in a year; and these seeds retain their viability for several years. It is often deformed and covered with whitish mould, caused by the fungal parasite, *Cystopus candidus* (Pers.) Lév., which is mainly restricted to this species.

The shepherd's purse contains a substance which causes contraction of the blood vessels. For this reason, it has been long used in folk medicine to stop internal bleeding. Its effectiveness in the healing of external wounds must also be mentioned. If taken in large quantities, it can be poisonous. During the First World War an effort was made to replace the scarce ergot fungus (*Claviceps purpurea* [Fr.] Tulasne) and the widely-used yellow pucoon (*Hydrastis canadensis* L.) by the shepherd's purse for pharmaceutical purposes. Both the above plants contained poisonous alkaloids, and stopped internal bleeding. It is also claimed that the fresh leaves of the shepherd's purse repel troublesome insects.

III—XI; ☉ — ☉;
5—40 cm.
Stem:
Erect, little
to much branched.
Leaves: Basal
rosette of lyrate
leaves; stem-
leaves lanceolate,
clasping the stem
at their base.
Flowers: Small,
white, forming
a long raceme.
Fruit: A triangular
pod or silicula,
with a remnant of
the style showing
as a short blunt
point.
Originally Eu.,
W. As., at present
almost cosm.

1 — flower,
2 — silicula

1

2

Annual Meadow Grass

Poa annua L.

The grass family
Graminae

The annual meadow grass is a typical representative of the huge genus *Poa*, whose members have an economic value as very important meadow grasses. This grass provides a fine and tasty fodder, but as it is diminutive, it is unproductive and is not used as cattle food. It grows in wasteland, by the roadside, in arable fields, gardens and even in the streets between paving stones. It is resistant to trampling, and is often the only plant growing in places where cattle are gathered. It also forms extensive growths on village greens where geese graze.

It can stand low temperatures and flowers throughout the winter if there is no snow, as does the common chickweed (*Stellaria media* [L.] Vill.). In a single year it can produce as many as three generations. Because of its resistant qualities and modest soil and climatic requirements, it is not surprising that, at present, it is widespread all over the temperate world; it has even been found on islands close to the Antarctic. It is not a troublesome weed as its shallow roots can be easily dislodged. The seeds need daylight to germinate well.

III—XI; ☉ — ☉;
5—25 cm; small tufts.
Roots: Fibrous.
Culms: Ascending.
Leaf-blades: Contracted at the tip.
Inflorescence: Panicles, elongated and triangular; spikelets of 3—5 florets, 3 mm long, green or yellow-green.
Glumes: Lower 1 — veined, upper 3 — veined.
Anthers: Up to 1 mm long. At present almost cosm.

1 — spikelet

1

Red Dead-nettle

Lamium purpureum L.

The dead-nettle
and mint family
Labiatae

The red dead-nettle can survive winter at various stages of growth and frequently blooms during mild spells even in the middle of winter. It grows in fields and gardens as a weed, on fallow and wasteland, near roads and fences. The flowers produce nectar. Apart from its usual flowers, which have a tubular corolla pollinated by insects, it sometimes produces inconspicuous flowers which do not open and, therefore, are self-pollinated. In this way, the plant can multiply even during unfavourable weather conditions. The ripe nutlet has a yellow, oily outgrowth at its base, which is a delicacy for ants. They transport the fruits to places which it might not reach without their help. Cattle avoid the red dead-nettle because of its unpleasant smell.

The perennial spotted dead-nettle (*L. maculatum* L.) is very similar to the red dead-nettle but is easily distinguished by the silvery-white band down the centre of each leaf. It grows in light woodland, alongside streams and rivers, by roadsides and in waste places.

III—IX; ☉—☉;
10—20 cm.
Stems: Short and ascending, unbranched, square in cross section.
Leaves: Petiolate, ovate, cordate, crenate-serrate.
Flowers:
In axils of bracts, purple-pink.
Calyx: With narrow, pointed teeth.
Corolla:
With straight tube and a hooded upper lip.
Stamens: 4.
Seeds: 4 nutlets.
Eu., As., introduced in N. Am.

1 — flower of the red dead-nettle,
2 — flower of the spotted dead-nettle

1

2

Kingcup, Marsh Marigold or May Blobs

Caltha palustris L.

The buttercup
family
Ranunculaceae

In spring the bright golden yellow flowers of the kingcup are the main ornament of marshy ground and prominent alongside streams and ponds, and in moist woodland clearings and meadows. If the weather is favourable, they can sometimes be seen at the beginning of autumn. The flowers are often visited by insects, which are attracted not only by pollen, as in the case of the anemone, but also by nectar, secreted from small depressions, one on either side of each carpel. Pollination is ensured by the vast number of visiting insects. The fruits are pod-like follicles, which ripen while they are still green. The seeds are spread by rain or floods.

Cattle avoid the kingcup as its juice, containing protoanemonine, like other members of the *Ranunculaceae*, has a sharp taste. However, since the kingcup has only a low percentage of this substance, only slight poisoning is caused. The kingcup was also well-known in the kitchen, as its unopened flower-buds preserved in vinegar were used to replace the true Mediterranean caper. Its juice was also employed for colouring butter.

III—V; 2↓;
10—50 cm.
Roots: Fibrous.
Stems: Ascending.
Leaves: Basal
long-stalked,
upper subsessile,
crenate.
Flowers:
Bright golden
yellow, glossy.
Fruits: Follicles,
narrowing into
a beak.
Eu., As., N. Am.

1 — follicles

Ground Ivy

Glechoma hederacea L.
(Syn. *Nepeta hederacea*)

The dead-nettle
and mint family
Labiatae

The ground ivy grows in thickets, woods and meadows, on grassy banks, in ditches, close to roads and at the foot of hedges, fences and walls. It spreads rapidly by its prostrate rooting stems. The flowers have usually 4 stamens, 2 long and 2 short, just like most of other members of the *Labiatae*.

Cattle usually avoid the ground ivy because of its aroma and bitter, spicy taste. The poisoning of horses has been recorded after they have eaten a large quantity of this plant. Its glandular hairs can cause a rash to sensitive skin. In olden days the ground ivy was used to cure diseases of the breathing tract, to get rid of coughs, and for bathing ulcerous wounds. It was also a vermifuge used for horses. Nowadays, it is still used in the countryside, where its young, spring leaves are added to soup, and make a tasty vegetable dish. A form with white variegated leaves is grown in gardens, particularly as a hanging basket plant.

IV—VI; ♃;
10—20 cm.
Stems: Creeping, branched, rooting at the nodes, flowering stem ascending.
Leaves: Opposite, stalked, reniform, crenate.
Corolla: Tubular, with two lobed lips, up to 2 cm long, purple-blue.
Fruits:
4 smooth nutlets.
Eu., As., introduced in N. Am.

1 — flower

1

Common Dandelion

Taraxacum officinale WEB.

The daisy family
Compositae

The common dandelion can be found in almost any kind of grassland, from dry hills to water meadows; it is also a weed of waste and arable land and in gardens. The yellow flower heads are made up of as many as 150 tiny strap-shaped florets. The calyx eventually changes into a parachute of hairs (pappus) which remains on the achenes (seeds) and serves for wind dispersal. This enables the dandelion to spread over considerable distances. The achenes can develop without pollination, and can even ripen on stems that were picked soon after the blossoms had faded. The plant is difficult to control as it has long taproots, which can produce new plants if they are cut or broken. The common dandelion is very useful, for its young leaves make a tasty salad when blanched, and the cooked green leaves are a substitute for spinach. The roots are used in some countries as a coffee substitute, and the flowers make a good wine. It has a wide application as a medicine and also provides valuable nectar for bees. The dandelion is a very variable plant and several hundreds of distinct forms or micro-species have been described.

IV—VI; ♃; 10—30 cm; produces white milky sap.
Leaves: In basal rosette, lanceolate, pinnate or deeply crenate.
Stems: Numerous, tubular, with solitary inflorescences.
Florets: Strap or tongue-shaped, yellow
Achenes: Grey-brown, narrowing into a long beak with pappus.
Eu., As., N. Am., at present almost cosm.

1 — ligulate flower,
2 — achene

1

2

Germander Speedwell

Veronica chamaedrys L.

The anthirrhinum
or figwort family
Scrophulariaceae

The germander speedwell is a common plant of
meadows and pastures; it grows by the roadside,
on hedgebanks, at the edges of woods, in thickets,
and in the sparse woods of lowland and mountain
slopes. It usually has beautiful, sky-blue flowers,
although, occasionally, they are pink, or white.
It is pollinated by insects, usually flies, but also
by various beetles and bees. The nectar, secreted
inside the flower, can be easily reached by insects
with a short proboscis, as the corolla-tube is
relatively short. In unfavourable weather conditions, the flowers can be self-pollinated. The
corolla, with two attached stamens, drops off soon
after pollination. The seeds are dispersed by ants,
or by the wind, and, sometimes, even by the rain.
One of the most outstanding features of the
germander speedwell, as opposed to other speedwells, are two rows of long white hairs on either
side of the rounded stem.

IV—VII; 2;
10—30 cm.
Stem: Prostrate,
the flowering
tips ascending.
Leaves:
Opposite, sessile,
lower short-
stalked, oval,
crenate serrate.
Flowers:
In racemes.
Corolla: Sky-blue.
Capsules:
Triangular-
cordate,
4 mm long.
Eu., As.

1 — a part of the
stem with two
rows of hairs,
2 — flower,
3 — capsule

1

2

3

Cowslip or Paigle
Primula veris L.

The primrose
family
Primulaceae

The cowslip, along with other spring plants, forms the herbaceous undergrowth of the hornbeam-oak forests in warm lowlands and on hillsides. In Britain however, it is commonly found in pastures and on grassy slopes, particularly in limey soils. It has yoke-yellow flowers with orange spots within the base of the corolla; the tubular calyx is slightly inflated. In mountainous regions, and, especially, in damp woods or woodland margins, it is replaced by the oxlip (*P. elatior* [L.] Hill), which has larger, paler yellow flowers and a narrower calyx appressed to the corolla-tube. The cowslip is used for medical purposes, and also contains vitamin C.

The cowslip produces two types of flowers on separate plants. The first or pin-eyed type has the style as long as the corolla-tube and the stigma has small elongated projections; the 5 short stamens are attached half-way down the corolla-tube and the pollen grains are small. The second or thrum-eyed type has a style reaching only midway up the corolla-tube and the stigma has short projections; the stamens are attached close to the mouth of the corolla-tube and the anthers carry large pollen grains. Large pollen grains usually germinate on the stigma with elongated projections, while the small grains germinate on the stigma with short projections. This phenomenon, of a varying length of the style in relation to other parts of flower, is called heterostyly. In this way the plant is effectively protected from self-pollination.

IV—V; ♃;
10—20 cm;
Leaves: In basal rosette, elongated, wrinkled, narrowed at the base.
Flowers: In umbel.
Calyx: Separated from the corolla-tube.
Petals: Yoke-yellow.
Corolla-tube: Longer than the calyx.
Ripe capsule: Oval and shorter than the calyx.
Eu., As.

1 — capsule

1

Common Violet

Viola riviniana RCHB.

There are 500 species of violets in the world, not including a large number of cultivated varieties and hybrids. The common violet is one of the relatively numerous species growing in light woods and, especially, in oak-hornbeam and oak-pine forests. It is called after August Quirinus Rivinus, Professor of Botany at Leipzig, who lived between 1652—1722. It resembles the pale wood violet (*V. reichenbachiana* Jord.), for which it is sometimes mistaken.

The relatively large, light purple flowers are unscented, but they attract insects in a different way. The lower petal narrows at the base and projects backwards into a short hollow spur, which contains nectar. Multi-seeded capsules burst into three valves when they ripen and, as each valve dries and contracts, the seeds are ejected several feet away. The common violet is a variable plant as to leaf and flower size. A small compact form, *V. r. minor*, is often found on dry grassy slopes or moorland.

IV—VI; $2\!\!\!\downarrow$;
5—20 cm;
Rhizome:
Creeping.
Stem: Ascending.
Leaves: Stalked, broadly cordate.
Flowers:
Pale violet,
1—2½ cm, with whitish, thick blunt spur about 5 mm long, having a notched apex.
Eu., As.

1 — bract

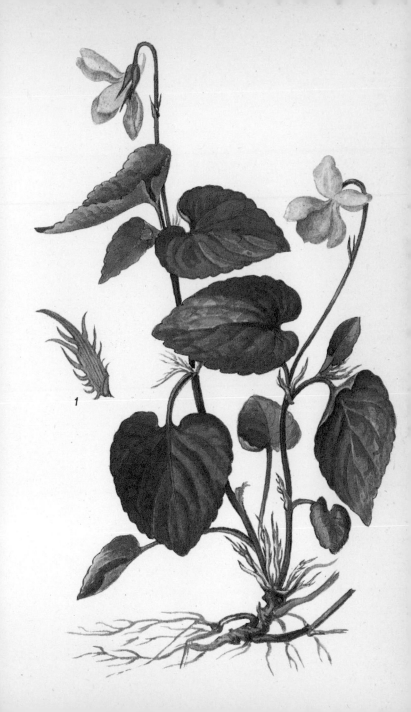

1

Sweet Vernal-grass
Anthoxanthum odoratum L.

The grass family
Graminae

The sweet vernal-grass is one of the first grasses to flower in spring. It grows in dry, to moderately damp, grassland, on slopes, in meadows, in light deciduous, oak and birch forests, in pine forests and on river banks. Cattle will graze on it, but its nutritional value is not high. When it occurs in large quantities, it can effect the fodder with its bitter taste. Freshly cut and drying plants emit a sweet, hay scent, caused by a substance called coumarin. This substance is also present in some other plants, especially in relatively rare grasses, such as the holy-grass (*Hierochloë australis* [Schrad.] Roem. et Schult.), the sweet woodruff (*Galium odoratum* [L.] Scop.) and the common melilot (*Melilotus officinalis* [L.] Lamk.). Because it contains coumarin, the sweet vernal-grass used to be mixed with tobacco to give it added aroma.

IV—VI; 2↓;
10—50 cm;
tufted grass with erect flowering stems.
Leaves:
Usually hairy.
Panicle: Spike-shaped, 2—5 cm long, yellow-green.
Spikelets:
One-flowered, with 2 stamens and 2 flexible stigmas.
Ovaries: Enclosed in lemmas.
Eu., As., western part of N. Af.; introduced in N. Am., Au.

1 — spikelet

1

Cuckoo Flower or Lady's Smock

Cardamine pratensis L.

The cabbage
family
Cruçiferae

In spring, blossoms of the cuckoo flower bathe water meadows, moist valleys, streamsides, river banks and around ponds in a lilac shade. The blossoms close and bend during rain and at night. Its relative profusion is not dependent only on seed propagation. For the cuckoo flower has an unusual ability to produce bud-like plantlets on its basal leaves, which root and form new plants. Seed production is also important, and large quantities are produced in a good season. The pod-like fruits (siliquae) rupture suddenly, throwing the seeds several feet away.

Balls of froth can be often noticed on the stems; they are called cuckoo's spit, or devil's saliva. They are formed by larvae of the meadow frog-hopper from the surplus juices sucked from the plants. Cuckoo flower is also one of the food plants of the lovely orange-tip butterfly. The flowers are rich in nectar, and the content of vitamin C in the leaves is very substantial, being five times higher than in lemons. The cuckoo flower can, therefore, be used as an antiscorbutant.

IV—VI; 2|;
15—35 cm.
Rhizome: Short.
Stem: Erect, slightly branched.
Leaves: Pinnate with rounded to linear leaflets with serrate or entire margins.
Flowers: In a terminal raceme.
Petals: Lilac with darker veins.
Siliquae: Long-stalked, up to 4 cm long.
Eu., As., N. Am.

1 — siliqua

1

Common Wood-sorrel

Oxalis acetosella L.

The wood-sorrel
family
Oxalidaceae

The wood-sorrel often produces extensive colonies in shady deciduous, mixed, or coniferous woods both in lowland and mountain areas. It indicates soils which have a plentiful supply of decaying organic matter. The whole plant contains a considerable amount of oxalic acid and its related salts. The acid flavour of its leaves seems to be refreshing, but, when eaten by children in large quantities, it can cause serious poisoning. Oxalic acid is harmful to the kidneys and heart. In spring, when there is general lack of green pasture, large quantities of the wood-sorrel can endanger cattle grazing in woods, and the effects can be deadly, especially in sheep.

The flowers of wood-sorrel close and bend downwards at night, whilst the clover-like leaf blades fold in half, and also hang down. This plant can be "put to sleep" even at midday, if it is covered with a hat, or deeply overshadowed in some other way. The capsules split when ripe, forming five side slots, through which the seeds are ejected up to several feet away.

IV—V; ♃;
5—15 cm.
Rhizome: Thin, creeping, leaves and flowering stems arising directly from it.
Leaves: Petiolate, trifoliate.
Flowers:
Solitary on long stalks with 5 white, pink or purplish tinted petals.
Capsules:
Up to 1 cm long.
Eu., As., N. Af., N. Am.

1 — immature capsule with ensheathing sepals

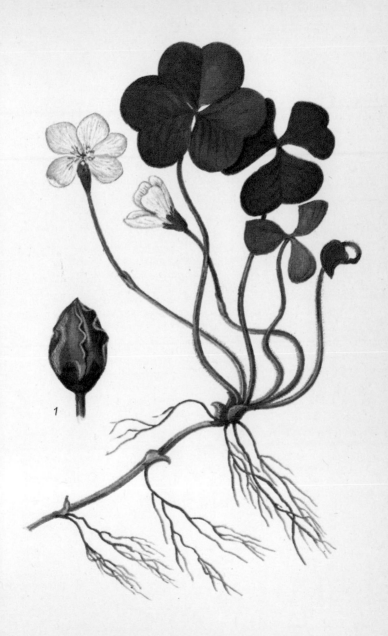

1

Field Penny-cress

Thlaspi arvense L.

The cabbage
family
Cruciferae

This plant has been given the name of penny-cress because of its fruit, its flattened rounded shape resembling a penny. There has been a lot of effort wasted in endeavouring to exterminate its unwelcome growth from agricultural land, but it continues to grow everywhere, often in abundance. If the oil, which is present in its seeds in the proportion of 24%—32% could be used, it would have some fodder value. However, because it smells strongly of garlic, as does the whole plant, it is avoided by herbivorous animals. If it is mixed with cattle food in large volume, especially with its ripe seeds, it can irritate the mucous membrane of the cattle's digestive tract and even cause slight poisoning. In any case, the milk and, especially, the butter produced from such milk, smells unpleasantly of garlic. This is caused by magnesium ether, which is also found in other plants of the cabbage family.

IV—VI (—X);
$\odot — \odot$;
10—40 cm;
glabrous plant.
Basal leaves:
Stalked, soon
withering.
Stem-leaves:
Distantly toothed,
clasp the stem.
Petals: 4 white,
twice as long as
4 sepals.
Fruits:
Broadly eliptic or
round siliculas
with winged
margins and
notched tips.
Eu., As.;
introduced
elsewhere.

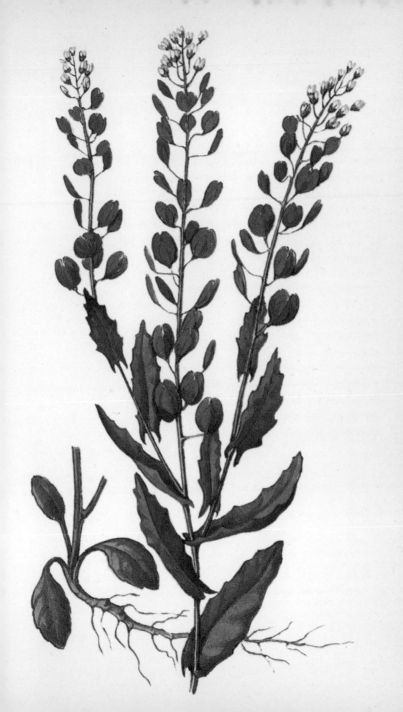

Sun Spurge

Euphorbia helioscopia L.

This annual weed was given its Latin name because of the fact that it continually turns its inflorescence towards the sun (*helios*, sun, and *skopein*, to look). It has been growing on cultivated ground ever since the early Stone Age. It is probably a native of the Mediterranean region, although today it is widespread in gardens, in fields and vineyards, by roadsides and in wasteland. The seeds are distributed in an interesting way. The dry three lobed capsules burst abruptly ejecting the seeds as far as one metre away from the parent plant. The seeds are covered with an intricate, raised network pattern, well worth viewing with a hand lens. Like other members of the family, the sun spurge contains a poisonous, white, milky juice, which causes inflammation of the digestive tract in domestic animals. It can also cause severe irritation, and even blindness, if it comes into contact with the eyes.

IV—X; ☉; 10—50 cm.
Stem: Erect, usually sparingly branched low down.
Leaves: Alternate, obovate, finely serrate at the tip; bracts beneath the flower similar to the leaves, but broader and paler green.
Inflorescence: Umbel, 5-rayed, each ray terminated by a flower and 3 branches each bearing further flowers.
Blossoms: Yellow-green.
Glands: Oval.
Capsules: Smooth.
Eu., As., N. Af.; elsewhere introduced.

1 — part of inflorescence, 2 — capsule

1

2

White Dead-nettle

Lamium album L.

The dead-nettle
and mint family
Labiatae

The white dead-nettle with leaves similar to those of the common stinging nettle (*Urtica dioica* L.*), often grows in similar places, which have a high content of nitrogenous substances in the soil, such as wasteland, thickets, hedgebanks, roadsides and thin woods. The blossoms are a-dapted to the visits of insect. The upper, hooded lip shields two long and two short stamens. Nectar is secreted at the bottom of the corolla-tube, which is covered internally with fine hair, and which prevents small insects from reaching the nectar. When bees or bumble-bees pollinate the flowers, they touch the anthers, shake the pollen on to their hairy bodies, and in this way transfer it to other flowers.

The white dead-nettle contains various medicinal substances, but usually only the white flowers are collected. This, and the subsequent drying process can be quite painstaking work, because the flowers easily turn brown. Nevertheless, its medicinal effects are reputed to be considerable, as it can be used as a sedative for neuritis, to regulate bowel activity, to sooth coughs or to cure inflamed wounds. The young leaves in spring can also be used as a spinach-like vegetable.

IV—IX; $2\!\!\downarrow$; 20—40 cm.
Rhizome: Creeping.
Stalks: Erect, unbranched, square in cross section.
Leaves: Opposite, petiolate, cordate, ovate, serrate.
Flowers: In the axils of leaf-like bracts.
Calyx: White, bell-shaped with narrow pointed teeth.
Corolla: 2-lipped with 4 stamens.
Fruit: 4 achenes.
Eu., As.; secondary N. Am.

1 — longitudinal cross-section of the flower,
2 — achenes

1

2

Meadow Buttercup

Ranunculus acris L.

The buttercup
family
Ranunculaceae

The glossy, golden-yellow blossoms of the meadow buttercup appear in meadows, damp pastures and ditches at the peak of spring. It is regarded as a common, unimportant plant. However, its dangerous side effects must not be underestimated. The whole plant contains protoanemonine, a highly irritating substance, which often causes skin inflammations difficult to heal. The mere pressure of its fresh leaves against a sensitive skin can, after a while, cause unpleasant blistering. Cattle avoid the meadow buttercup, although hay containing this plant is not dangerous, as protoanemonine loses its poisonous character during drying. The poison penetrates the milk of poisoned cows, and, if fresh plants are eaten by mistake by human beings, they can cause strong inflammation of the mouth, stomach and intestine, accompanied by sickness, convulsion, faintness and copious salivation. At the same time, protoanemonine has antibacterial properties, similar to antibiotics; but, unfortunately, it has so far not been possible to use it owing to its irritant qualities. A double-flowered form, *R. a.* "Flore Pleno", is often cultivated in gardens.

V—X; ♃;
30—100 cm.
Rhizome: Short, thick.
Stem: Erect, profusely branched.
Basal leaves: Petiolate, palmately 5—7 lobed.
Upper stem-leaves: Sessile, cut into narrow segments.
Flower stems: Not furrowed.
Flowers: 1.5—2.5 cm in diameter, 5 green sepals, 5 petals; followed by rounded pale brown achenes with a short hooked beak.
Eu., W. Siberia

1 — achenes

1

Ox-eye Daisy or Moon-Daisy
Chrysanthemum leucanthemum L.

The daisy family
Compositae

The ox-eye daisy grows in meadows and pastures, on banks and grassy slopes. The older plants especially are unwelcome in haymaking, as their stems are excessively tough, and disliked by cattle. Its way of pollination is interesting: in each tiny floret the stamens are fused together, forming a tube; the stamen bursts into this tube while the floret is still closed, and the ripe pollen forms a layer above the stigma. When the flower opens the stigma pushes the pollen out of the anther tube ready to be picked up by visiting insects. When the stigma is well above the tube and loose pollen, it expands the two stigmatic lobes and is ready to receive pollen from another flower. If cross-pollination does not occur, these lobes bend back in a circle so that they touch the loose pollen and are thus self-pollinated.

The larger, but closely related, shasta daisy (*Chrysanthemum maximum*) sometimes escapes from gardens. This Pyrenean plant has many handsome forms including those with full, double flowers.

V—X; $2\vert$;
20—60 cm.
Rhizome: Short.
Stem: Erect,
simple or
sparingly
branched.
Leaves: Basal
obovate, petiolate
upper oblong,
sessile, crenate.
Terminal heads:
2.5—5 cm across.
Ray-florets:
Strap-shaped,
white.
Disc-florets:
Cylindrical,
golden yellow.
Achenes:
Cylindrical
with 5—10 ribs.
Eu., As.;
introduced in
N. Am., N. Z.

1 — ray-floret,
2 — cylindrical
disc-floret

1

2

Ragged Robin

Lychnis flos-cuculi L.

The carnation
family
Caryophyllaceae

Having bright reddish-pink flowers, the ragged robin inhabits mainly damp woods, meadows and marshy ground where it sometimes grows in large quantities. Its Latin name is derived from the vivid colouring of its flowers; *lichnos* means in Greek a light or a lantern. The flowers secrete plenty of nectar, and, because the corolla is relatively short, its blossom can be pollinated by insects with only a short proboscis. Close observation reveals not only the usual bisexual flowers, but also those with anthers alone, or only pistils, which after pollination turn into capsules. The ripe capsule opens at the top and contains numerous seeds, which are distributed each time the wind sways the stem from side to side. Balls of froth can often be found at the leaf axils; it is produced by the larvae of a sucking insect, the meadow frog-hopper, from the juice sucked from the plant; a similar phenomenon can be noticed on the cuckoo flower, and many other plants in both the wild and cultivation.

V—VII; ♃;
30—70 cm.
Stem: Erect, glabrous.
Leaves: Opposite, sessile oblanceolate.
Calyx: Cup-shaped with 5 pointed lobes.
Petals: 5, rose-red, occasionally white, deeply cleft into 4 narrow segments.
Capsule: With numerous seeds. Eu., As.

1 — capsule

1

Ribwort
Plantago lanceolata L.

The plantain
family
Plantaginaceae

The ribwort grows profusely in meadows and pastures, by the roadside, in ditches and on wasteland. Its seeds have an absorbant coat, which becomes mucilaginous very quickly when wetted, so that, after rain, it easily adheres to human or animal feet and to cart wheels, and, in this way, can be easily carried over long distances. Young plants eaten by live stock can cause slight diarrhoea. It used to be added to clover to prevent flatulence in cattle. It has been used in herbal medicine with an overproduction of phlegm. The juice extracted from its freshly-gathered leaves was formerly applied to wounds to promote rapid healing. For other purposes its leaves must be quickly and carefully dried, otherwise they easily turn brown or black.

V—IX; ♃; 10—40 cm.
Rhizome: Short.
Leaves: In basal rosette, 3—7 nerved, entire, lanceolate.
Stem: Furrowed lengthways, terminated by a dense spike of tiny flowers.
Calyx and corolla: Brown and papery.
Stamens: Longer than corolla, with large, white, prominent anthers.
Fruit: A capsule which splits transversely, the top forming a lid which falls away. Eu., As; introduced almost all over the world.

1 — capsule with lid

1

Water Forget-me-not

Myosotis scorpioides L.
(Syn. *M. palustris* [L.] NATH.)

The borage
family
Boraginaceae

V—X; 2↓;
15—45 cm.
Rhizome:
Creeping.
Stems: Erect or
decumbent,
angular at the
base.
Leaves: Alternate,
oblong-lanceolate,
narrowing to
a winged petiole,
upper sessile.
Flowers: In cymes,
sky-blue, pink
when young,
with a small
yellow eye.
Fruits: 4 glossy
black achenes.
Eu., As., N. Af.,
N. Am.

The beauty of the sky-blue flowers of the water forget-me-not is generally appreciated, but a close examination of the opening buds reveals that they are not blue, but pink. The change of colour takes place with the gradual development of the blossom. The petals contain pigment consisting of anthocyanins, and its colour depends on the acidity of the cell juice; the colour varies in an acid, neutral or alkaline environment. The stages between red, violet and blue can also be noticed in other plants, the flowers of which contain anthocyanins, such as the common lungwort (*Pulmonaria officinalis* L.), the spring vetchling (*Lathyrus vernus* [L.] Bernh.) and others. The nature of this phenomenon is revealed if ants on an anthill are teased with a blue flower, as the colour of that flower then turns red.

The water forget-me-not grows in great profusion on river banks, in damp meadows and in woods, often in association with the kingcup (*Caltha palustris* L.*). There are several other closely related species of water forget-me-not, notably *M. secunda* and *M. caespitosa*, which differ in flower size, degree and type of hairiness and habit of growth.

1 — flower

1

Perennial Rye-grass or Ray-grass

Lolium perenne L.

The grass family
Graminae

The rye-grass is one of the most valuable pasture grasses. It tolerates being trodden on, and thrives when regularly cut or grazed. It is, therefore, well suited for playgrounds and airports, where it forms continuous, firm, springy turf. If it is untended on loose soil, it can easily become sparse. It thrives in the damp, maritime climate of the temperate zones. That is why it has been used in England for sown pasture since the 17th century. In more recent times, plant breeders have produced superior, more vigorous selections to suit the needs of both farmers and gardeners.

Nowadays, the darnel (*L. temulentum* L.), its annual relative, is only rarely seen in corn fields. Its spikes sometimes contain the parasitic fungus known as ergot, which produces a poisonous alkaloid. In the past this poison used to get into flour, causing drowsiness, headaches and sickness. In some countries monks used secretly to add the ergot grains to malt and hops to make their beer more intoxicating.

V—VIII; ♃;
20—50 cm;
tufted grass.
Stems: Erect, glabrous.
Leaves: Flat, 3—6 mm wide, with short ligules.
Spikelets: Composed of yellowish green 4—14 florets.
Glumes: Awnless.
Stamens: 3.
Seed: Grain, 5—7 mm long, tightly enclosed in hardened lemma.
Eu., As., N. Af.; introduced N. Am., Au.

1 — spikelet

1

Mouse-ear Hawkweed
Hieracium pilosella L.

The daisy family
Compositae

The mouse-ear hawkweed is one of the most common species of hawkweed. It grows in light woodland glades, including pine forests, and in forest margins. However, it is more characteristic of dry sandy soils, dry limestone pastures and heathland. Its long, leafy, stem-like stolons which root in as they spread enable the formation of large colonies of this plant. It often grows as a pioneer in dry sandy or chalky areas, where other plants cannot exist.

The hawkweed genus (*Hieracium* L.) has about 5,000 species and forms many of which are members of the European flora. It is an actively evolving genus with many variable species, which readily mutate and are then difficult to identify precisely.

V—IX; ♃;
5—20 cm.
Leaves:
In basal rosette, obovate, hairy, white tomentose beneath (stolon leaves usually much narrower).
Stems: With solitary pale yellow flower heads.
Flowers:
Outer strap-shaped florets often red striped.
Achenes: Purple-black, 2 5 mm long.
Eu., As.

1 — achene

1

Field Bindweed or Cornbine

Convolvulus arvensis L.

The morning
glory or
bindweed family
Convolvulaceae

The field bindweed belongs to the group of very troublesome weeds inhabiting fields and gardens. It can wind its stems round those of a cultivated crop, often so densely as to smother and choke young plants. It grows in abundance on fallow and wasteland, on banks, along roadsides, in ditches and on pastureland. Its seeds retain their viability for over 20 years, but propagation by this method is of small account when compared with its underground, creeping rootstocks. These roots penetrate to a depth of several metres and branch profusely. Because of this characteristic, bindweed can prove useful in certain circumstances, for it does not need fertile soils, is able to withstand drought, and thus helps to prevent the erosion of banks and dikes.

Substances found in its roots have laxative properties, which explain the use of bindweed in folk medicine.

The growing top of the plant follows a circular movement, the plant winding round the nearest stem or similar support. At the height of its growing season, bindweed stems can encircle the diameter of its support rapidly; as much as one centimetre in about an hour. The direction of such circular movements is clockwise when looking down on the plant. Some other climbing plants, such as the runner-bean, rotate in the opposite direction.

V—IX; ♃;
20—120 cm.
Stems:
Scrambling
or climbing.
Leaves: Alternate,
petiolate, oblong
or ovate, hastate
or sagittate,
entire.
Flowers:
Stalked, in the
axils of leaves.
Calyx: With
5 segments.
Corolla: Wide,
funnel-shaped,
1.5—2.5 cm
long, white or
pink.
Capsules:
Globular, usually
with 4 seeds.
Native of the
Mediterranean
region as
far as the Near
East; today
almost cosm.

1 — capsule

1

Birdsfoot-trefoil
or **Bacon and Eggs**
Lotus corniculatus L.

The pea family
Leguminosae

The birdsfoot-trefoil, one of the most common members of the pea family, grows in pastures, meadows, on banks and sunny slopes, and sometimes even in woodland clearings. Like the majority of members of this family, the birdsfoot-trefoil has nodules scattered over its roots. They are inhabited by bacteria which assimilate nitrogen. This is one of the rare ways in which plants can make use of nitrogen in the air. Theophrastus, an ancient Greek scientist (370—285 B.C.), discovered that members of the *Leguminosae* enrich the soil, but the method, the isolation of the bacteria in the root nodules, was not fully understood until the end of the 19th century.

The birdsfoot-trefoil is considered to be a good fodder plant both for cutting and grazing; in some parts of Europe it is sometimes added to clover-grass seed. When the pods are fully ripe, and during dry warm weather, they burst and eject the seeds over a wide area.

A handsome and profusely blooming double-flowered form of birdsfoot-trefoil (*L. c.* "Flore Pleno") is sometimes cultivated in gardens.

V—XI; ♃;
10—40 cm.
Stems:
Creeping
or decumbent.
Leaves: Composed
of 5 leaflets;
lowest leaves
similar to bracts.
Flowers:
Deep yellow,
often streaked
with red, 3 to
7 in each head.
Fruits: Cylindrical
pods up to 3 cm
long.
Eu., N., and
E. Af., SW. As.;
elsewhere
introduced.

1 — flower,
2 — pods

Silverweed

Potentilla anserina L.

Silverweed often grows in large patches by the roadside, in farmyards and, often, in places where geese graze. It can be also found in ditches, on river banks, in pastures and in damp places, which are occasionally subjected to flooding. It can become a troublesome weed in damp fields as it spreads by seed, or vegetatively by its creeping stolons. The thick ground cover this plant can produce does not allow other species to germinate. Nevertheless, it is an attractive plant with its silvery, silky-haired, ferny leaves and bright, yellow flowers.

The flowering stems were formerly used in the treatment of stomach and intestinal disorders, and for bathing wounds slow to heal. It contains a substance which gives it an astringent taste. The herbal properties of the silverweed are also shared by the creeping cinquefoil (*Potentilla reptans* L.), an allied plant which has palmate leaves divided into five leaflets, and which grows profusely in ditches, by the roadside, on grassy slopes, and on waste ground.

V—VIII; ♃;
10—30 cm or more.
Rhizome:
Thick, producing creeping, leafy, rooting stolons.
Leaves: Odd-pinnate.
Flowers:
2 cm across, solitary on long stalks with 5 golden yellow petals and several stamens.
Achenes:
Rounded, smooth.
Eu., As.;
introduced N. Am., Au., N. Z.

White or Dutch Clover
Trifolium repens L.

The pea family
Leguminosae

As with the majority of the members of the pea family, symbiotic, nodule-inhabiting bacteria of the genus *Rhizobium* live on the roots of the white clover. They, similarly, absorb nitrogen from the air, and in this way enrich the soil. This clover species is often sown in meadows and pastures, by itself or mixed with rye-grass. It is a valuable pasture plant and several improved cultivated varieties exist. An analysis of this plant revealed that some strains contain hydrocyanic acid, which can cause slight poisoning in large quantities. Pigs especially have been observed to suffer in this respect.

The majority of clovers are pollinated by bumble-bees, but, as the white clover has a shorter corolla-tube than the others, its flowers are often visited by honey bees, which can easily reach the nectar at the base of the flower. That is why this plant is of great value for honey production. The small, shiny seeds can pass through the digestive tract of animals without causing any damage. So white clover can easily be spread by animal droppings.

V—X; 2↓;
5—20 cm;
Stems: Rooting, creeping or decumbent.
Leaves: Trifoliate, petiolate with large stipules.
Flower heads: Made up of numerous florets.
Calyx: 10-veined.
Corolla: White or pink, occasionally purplish.
Fruit: A pod, 1—6 seeds.
Originally perhaps Eu., today found in all continents.

1 — flower

1

Ground Elder, Goutweed or **Bishop's Weed**

Aegopodium podagraria L.

The carrot
family
Umbelliferae

Ground elder grows along the banks of streams and rivers, and in damp forests; and often forms continuous carpets in orchards beneath the shade of trees, where it smothers out the grass. It is a common and unwelcome weed in gardens. Digging tends to spread even more its thin, creeping, profusely-branching, brittle rootstocks, which can grow to a length of about 50 cm every year, and each segment of which can form a new plant. It prefers fertile, relatively moist soil with a high nitrogen content.

The flower's odour attracts insects, especially bees, so ground elder can be classified as a source of honey. Fresh, young leaves can be used for salads or cooked like spinach. They contain a high percentage of vitamin C, especially when mature during the summer. A form with variegated leaves is sometimes grown purposefully in gardens.

V—VIII; ♃;
50—80 cm;
Rhizomes: Thin, branching.
Stems: Erect, branched, hollow.
Leaves: Usually with 1 to 2, trifoliate ovate, serrate segments.
Inflorescence: Umbels without bracteoles.
Flowers: White or pinkish.
Fruit: Ribbed schizocarp.
Eu., As.; introduced in N. Am.

1 — flower.
2 — double fruit (schizocarp)

1

2

Bladder Campion

Silene vulgaris (MOENCH) GARCKE
(Syn. *S. cucubalus* WIBEL)

The carnation
family
Caryophyllaceae

The most outstanding features of this plant are its ash-grey foliage and its striking, inflated calyx. The Latin name *cucubalus* means pigeon's craw. It is derived from the bladder campion's resemblance to *Cucubalus baccifer* L., an allied plant of the same family with berry-like fruits eaten by pigeons. The depth of the calyx and the enclosed corolla tube allows only those nocturnal moths with a long proboscis to reach its excretions of nectar.

The bladder campion grows on dry slopes, by the roadsides, on banks and rocks, in quarries and in the light woods of lowlands and highlands. In the past it was used for medicinal purposes. Of the substances it contains only the soapy saponins are worth mentioning, and they are not present in sufficient quantity to be worthwhile extracting.

V—X; ♃;
20—70 cm.
Stems: Erect, branching, glabrous.
Leaves: Lanceolate to ovate, entire, glabrous, ash-gray green.
Flowers: In cymes.
Calyx: Inflated, glabrous, with a network of veins.
Petals: Five, white, 2-lobed.
Capsule: Enclosed by the calyx, ovoid opening at the top.
Seeds: With short sharp tubercles.
Eu., As., N. Af.

1 — capsule

1

Field Poppy
Papaver rhoeas L.

The poppy
family
Papaveraceae

The field poppy is one of the most attractive weeds and has been many times portrayed by painters. Because of improved methods of cleaning grain and the seeds of other farm crops, it is slowly disappearing from the fields, despite the fact that one plant can produce as many as 50,000 seeds. It spread out from its probable original location in the Near East and has been growing in fields ever since the early Stone Age. It is now found on fallowland, banks and wasteland all over the temperate world. Field poppy is very variable in the shape and hairiness of its leaves and the colour of its flowers. The Shirley poppies grown in gardens were derived from this species by the Rev. W. Wilks, who found a white, red edged mutant, and bred and selected from it. The field poppy contains, especially in its flower, poisonous alkaloids which can be harmful to people and animals. Its petals were used in the past as a cough medicine. They were also used as a substitute for tea. Its seeds contain 44% oil, so flour made from badly-cleaned corn with a high content of poppy seeds is yellowish and quickly deteriorates.

V—VII; ⊙; 25—80 cm.
Stem: Erect, unbranched or slightly branching, hairy.
Leaves: Pinnatisect.
Flowers: With 2 sepals and 4 red petals up to 5 cm long.
Filaments: Slender.
Stigma: With 6—18 lobes.
Capsule: Obovoid, over 2 cm long.
Near Asia; introduced almost all over the world.

1 — capsule

1

Cornflower or Bluebottle

Centaurea cyanus L.

The daisy family
Compositae

The cornflower was once the companion of all field plants, especially corn. Nowadays it is much rarer owing to improved methods of harvesting and cleaning corn and other grain crops. It was probably a native of the Mediterranean and the Orient, and became widespread in prehistoric Europe, later spreading to other parts of the world. Its fruits have been found with corn grains in pile-dwellings in Switzerland and elsewhere.

The cornflower belongs to that triad of popular field weeds including the field poppy (*Papaver rhoeas* L.*) and corn cockle (*Agrostemma githago* L.), which is today a rarity in many areas. Cornflower seeds, under favourable conditions, can germinate in autumn, as soon as they are ripe, and they retain their viability for several years. The flowers contain a beautiful blue dye based upon the pigment cyanin. This is soluble in water, and is used to colour perfumes, wool, aromatic spices and even Champagne wines. The florets, forming the outer row in each flower head, were formerly used in herbal medicine for making lotions to cure eye inflammations. The plant can cause digestive troubles in farm animals if it is mixed in large quantities with their food.

VI—IX; ⊙;
30—60 cm
Stem: Erect, usually sparsely branched.
Leaves: Linear-lanceolate or linear, lower leaves pinnatifid.
Flowers: Terminal heads with toothed bracts, outer blue florets larger than the central ones.
Seeds: Achenes, smoothly downy, with a brush-like tuft of reddish hairs. Mediterranean, Orient; introduced almost cosm.

1 — lingulate floret,
2 — achene

1

2

Wild Radish or White Charlock

Raphanus raphanistrum L.

The cabbage
family
Cruciferae

The wild radish is one of the most widely distributed and most troublesome annual field weeds. Several hundred, sometimes over 2,000, seeds ripen on one plant; they retain their germinating ability for many years under ideal conditions. Seeds discovered deep in the soil had lasted viably for over 50 years. It is often mistaken for the charlock or wild mustard (*Sinapis arvensis* L.*), from which it differs by the colour of the flower, the shape of the calyx and fruit and its preference for the more acid soils. It often grows in mountain regions with harsher climatic conditions. It is harmful to corn, as the amount of nutriments and water it consumes is several times higher than the amount required by the cultivated plants. When in bloom, fields overgrown with the yellow form of this weed look as if the wild radish had been planted there on purpose. Its oily seeds can provide a useful oil, but, mixed with poorly cleaned corn, can lead to the production of a low-quality flour.

VI—VIII (—X); ☉; 20—50 cm. *Stem:* Erect, branched. *Leaves:* Lower pinnatifid, upper undivided, unevenly crenate. *Sepals:* Ascending. *Petals:* Sulphur yellow, white or lilac, often with darker veins. *Fruit:* A loment, with constrictions between individual seeds, breaking into 1-seeded joints. Eu., elsewhere introduced.

1 — flower,
2 — loment

Charlock or Wild Mustard

Sinapis arvensis L.

The charlock, like the wild radish (*Raphanus raphanistrum* L.*), is a widespread, persistent, annual field weed. Its seeds can retain their viability over a long period of time, so that, even after several years of fighting to control it, the dormant seeds are brought up to the surface through ploughing, and are able to germinate. When a field is overgrown with this weed, it is yellow in colour, which gives the impression that the charlock is really the cultivated plant. In reality, only its related species are cultivated, such as the white mustard, for mustard production, and other species for oil extraction. Successful control of the charlock depends on a sensible crop rotation plan and the use of modern herbicides. Its seeds, like the seeds of the wild radish, can provide lubricating oil. Cattle food containing this plant is unsuitable as food. As one of the nectar producing plants, the charlock is much frequented by bees.

VI—VIII (—X); ○; 20—50 cm.
Stem: Erect, branched.
Leaves: Undivided or pinnatifid, irregularly crenate.
Sepals: 4, spreading.
Petals: 4, rich bright yellow.
Siliqua: Glabrous or pubescent, slightly constricted when ripe.
Beak: Shorter than the siliqua.
Eu., W. As.; elsewhere introduced.

1 — flower,
2 — siliqua

1

2

Common Stonecrop
or **Wall-pepper**
Sedum acre L.

The fleshy leaves, containing water-storage tissue, enable the common stonecrop to grow in dry and parched places. It can be found on sunny slopes, banks, rocks, screes, sand-dunes and on walls. Its light seeds, distributed by the wind, often settle on high walls, and even on roofs.

The juice it contains has a sharp, burning taste, and animals avoid the plant. It can cause the inflammation and blistering of human skin, and disorders in the digestive tract of domestic animals, especially in their intestines. In former ages, it was used in folk medicine to lower blood pressure and to heal external ulcers and skin diseases.

Somewhat similar, but with grey-green leaves and white or pink tinged flowers, is the English stonecrop. It has a western distribution in Europe, often being found in maritime areas on sand-dunes, cliffs, walls and dry grassy slopes. Its botanical name, *Sedum anglicum* Huds., denotes that it was first found and described in Britain.

VI—VII; ♃; 5—10 cm; dense mat-forming plant. *Leaves:* Fleshy, flat above, rounded on the underside, 3—5 mm long, sessile. *Flowers:* Starry, yellow, in branched inflorescences with 5 yellow, pointed petals and 10 stamens. *Fruit:* Star-shaped, formed of several pointed carpels. Eu., N. Af.; introduced in N. Am., N. Z.

1 — fruit

1

Stinging or Common Nettle

Urtica dioica L.

The nettle
family
Urticaceae

Few plants have so effective a defence against herbivorous animals as the stinging nettle. Its stem and leaves are covered with stinging hairs which terminate in a small head covered by a silicified, cellular membrane. As soon as a hair is even gently touched, the fragile end breaks off and sticks in to the skin, injecting the stinging fluid from the cell. It contains histamine and other substances, which cause skin rash. On the other hand, there are animals for whom the stinging hairs are not harmful, and these, almost without exception, feed only on stinging nettles. Such animals are mainly caterpillars of some of the very loveliest butterflies, such as the red admiral, peacock, small tortoiseshell, map butterfly and others.

The stinging nettle was once used as a medical cure in the treatment of rheumatism. The young, spring nettle leaves not only provide food for goslings and ducklings, but also make an excellent substitute for spinach when cooked. Young nettles contain a considerable amount of vitamin C, provitamin A and an abundance of chlorophyll. The stinging nettle was once used in the textile industry because of its strong bast fibres.

VI—IX; $\natural$;
30—140 cm;
dioecious plant.
Rhizome:
Creeping,
branched.
Stems: Erect.
Leaves:
Opposite,
petiolate,
obovate, serrate,
acuminate with
bracts; stinging
hairs occur on
stems and leaves.
Inflorescence: On
axillary panicle,
consisting of
tiny, yellow-green
unisexual florets
with 4 segments.
Achenes: Rounded,
about 1.2 mm
across.
Today almost
cosm.

1 — male flower,
2 — female flower

118

2

1

Scarlet Pimpernel or Shepherd's Weather-glass

Anagallis arvensis L.

The primrose
family
Primulaceae

The scarlet pimpernel is a small plant with beautiful, vermilion-red, or, occasionally, pink or lilac flowers, which grows as a weed in fields, on fallowland, wasteground and in gardens. Its spherical capsules, which open transversely, contain as many as 40 small seeds; the total number on one plant may be from several hundred to two thousand. It is not however dangerous as a weed. Much rarer is *Anagallis arvensis* subspecies *foemina* with bright blue flowers and long pointed calyx teeth. It is difficult to determine its native country, since it has been growing on cultivated soil for a long time, and today has spread over almost the whole temperate world.

The substances it contains, and their properties, have not yet been thoroughly investigated, but it is quite clear that it is a poisonous plant, the seeds being especially dangerous. It has been used to cure insect stings since antiquity; and superstition ascribes to it the power to cure madness, and even the magic force to communicate with spirits.

VI—IX; ⊙;
6—30 cm.
Stems: Square in cross section.
Leaves: Procumbent, opposite, sessile, ovate, entire, dotted on the underside.
Flowers: With slender stalks, red, occasionally blue.
Capsules: Spherical, opening transversely, the top half falling away.
Eu., As., Af; today almost cosm.

1 — flower,
2 — capsule

Meadow Vetchling

Lathyrus pratensis L.

The stems of the meadow vetchling sometimes form thick colonies in ditches, in meadows and hedgerows, at the edges of woods, and in thickets. The flexible stems sometimes grow to a considerable height (120 cm has been recorded), provided they have a firm support to which they can cling with their tendrils. The plant stays green during mild winters, but new flowering stems arise from the rootstock each year. Infusions made from the stems and leaves have been recommended in the past as a soothing remedy for coughs and chronic bronchitis. The meadow vetchling is not considered positively poisonous, although related species can cause poisoning. For example, *Lathyrus sativus* L., once quite common in central Europe and used as a fodder crop, can cause paralysis, and respiratory trouble in people and animals. Related domestic vetchlings have not yet been exhaustively analysed.

VI—VII; ♃;
20—80 cm.
Rhizome: Slender.
Stems: Ascending, scrambling or climbing, angled.
Leaves: With one pair of lanceolate leaflets and a branched tendril.
Racemes: 3—12 flowered, one-sided.
Flowers: Yellow, 1.5—2 cm long.
Pods: Somewhat flattened, straight sided.
Eu., As., N. and E. Af.

1 — flower,
2 — pod

1

2

Self-heal

Prunella vulgaris L.

The dead-nettle
and mint family
Labiatae

Self-heal grows in meadows, by the roadside, in light woodland, on banks and in ditches both of lowland and highland areas. It thrives best in moist fertile soils but is tolerant of a wide range of growing conditions, even surviving in close cut lawns.

Its flowers are violet-blue, occasionally white or pink. Two longer and two shorter stamens are hidden under the upper lip. Insects trying to reach the nectar secreted deep down in the flower inevitably shake off the pollen on to their bodies, and so transfer it to other flowers. Self-pollination is also possible, if the flower is not pollinated by external agents. The flowers are usually bisexual, but sometimes flowers with aborted stamens can be found. Somewhat less common is the related *Prunella laciniata*, a more robust species with toothed or deeply cut stem leaves and white flowers. Forms of this with pink or pale blue-violet flowers are sometimes cultivated in gardens.

VI—IX; ♃;
5—25 cm.
Stems: Ascending,
square in cross
section, thinly
branched.
Leaves:
Opposite,
petiolate, ovate,
entire.
Flowers:
In oblong heads,
violet-blue,
10—14 mm long
with a hooded
upper lip.
Fruit:
4 shiny achenes.
Eu., As., N. Af.;
elsewhere
introduced.

1 — flower

Sheep's Sorrel

Rumex acetosella L.

The rhubarb
and dock family
Polygonaceae

Sheep's sorrel is a good indicator of poor, sandy, acid soils. However, it needs plenty of light to thrive well. It often grows on banks, near roads, on fallow land, in arable fields as a weed, in dry pine forests, on moorland and rocky slopes. It spreads profusely by seeds, of which several thousand can be produced by one plant, but its vegetative growth is even more extensive. Its extensive root system forms numerous buds which give rise to new plants. It is sometimes possible to get rid of this weed by applying lime to the soil, and by deep ploughing.

The inconspicuous flowers are pollinated by the wind. Sheep's sorrel is a very variable species, the tiny, narrow leaved forms being given the separate name of *Rumex tenuifolius* (Wallr.) Löve. It thrives in the poorest, driest soils. A large amount of the sheep's sorrel in fodder can cause illness to domestic animals, and a subsequent drop in milk production.

VI—IX; ♃;
10—30 cm.
Stems: Erect or ascending, sometimes branched.
Leaves: Stalked, oblanceolate or linear with hastate, spreading base.
Flowers: Unisexual, dioecious, with 6 persistent floral segments, the 3 inner ones enclosing the achenes.
Achenes: Triangular, light brown. Today cosm.

1 — achene

Toadflax

Linaria vulgaris MILL.

The antirrhinum
or figwort family
Scrophulariaceae

The toadflax has been given its name because of the similarity of its leaves to those of the true flax, but it is, in fact, not related in any way. It grows in ditches, along roads, on banks, on wasteland, in pastures, and in fields and gardens as a weed. It is well adapted for life in dry places, as its leaves are covered with fine, waxy scales, which prevent an excessive evaporation of water. The snapdragon-like flowers are also interesting. The receptacle at the base of the pistil secretes an abundance of nectar, which accumulates at the bottom of a long, slender spur. This nectar is only accessible to insects with a long proboscis, and strong enough to open the closed, mouth-like flower. Bumble bees often get round this problem simply by biting through the spur to reach the nectar. One plant can produce as many as 20,000 seeds, but they often fail to ripen, as the capsules are frequently damaged by insect parasites. The plant was formerly used as a medicinal herb; particularly its roots are said to stimulate digestion and are also used to promote sweating.

VI—IX; 2┤;
20—50 cm.
Stems: Erect, sometimes sparingly branched, glabrous.
Leaves: Grey-green, alternate, dense, linear-lanceolate, entire.
Flowers: In a terminal raceme, with a spur up to 3 cm long, sulphur yellow, with an orange spot on the mouth.
Capsule: Ovoid.
Seeds: Winged.
Eu., W. As.

1 — flower,
2 — capsule

1

2

Yarrow or Milfoil
Achillea millefolium L.

The daisy family
Compositae

Yarrow grows in dry meadows, on grassy, sunny slopes, at the edges of woods, by roadsides and on banks. It absorbs large amounts of nutriments from the soil, and so exhausts it appreciably. Its scientific name is not derived from the legendary Trojan hero, but from an ancient Greek doctor called Achillos, who is said to have cured a seriously wounded warrior called Teleph with it. Yarrow belongs to a group of generally recognized herbs. It is reputed to stimulate the secretion of gastric juices, to dispel lack of appetite, soothe coughs and slow down internal bleeding. Its stems and leaves have been used in the preparation of baths to cure ulcerous wounds and skin rashes. Yarrow silicon can also cure inflammation, but excessive use is not advised, as it can sometimes cause headache and dizziness. Yarrow is also useful when added to fodder, as it helps digestion, but only young shoots should be used for this purpose, and only in small quantities.

VI—X; ♃;
20—50 cm.
Rhizome:
Creeping.
Stems: Erect,
branching into
a flattened
inflorescence.
Leaves: Fern-like,
lanceolate,
2—3 pinnate.
Flowers: In small
heads forming
corymbs.
Ray-florets:
Rounded,
toothed,
white or pinkish.
Disc-florets:
Tubular, white.
Achenes: Silver-
grey, glabrous.
Eu., As.;
introduced in
N. Am., Au.,
N. Z.

1 — head,
2 — ray-floret,
3 — tubular disc-
floret

Dwarf Mallow

Malva neglecta WALLR.

For centuries, man in the course of cultivation has been incidentally treading into the mud the fruits of the dwarf mallow, which are colloquially known as "cheeses"; when the mud is dried out these seeds are further scattered. The young, fresh leaves contain relatively high percentages of vitamin C and provitamin A. The dwarf mallow is a very useful herb, because it contains a mucilaginous substance which is said to heal inflammations of the stomach and intestine and ulcerous skin diseases.

Today, it can be found in grassland and waste places, by roadsides, and especially close to manure and compost heaps. Its liking for soils rich in nitrogen is not incidental; it substantiates the fact that this plant moved with man to Europe long ago from its original homeland in Asia Minor and the eastern Mediterranean. Almost as common is the much larger common mallow (*Malva sylvestris* L.) with showy rose-purple flowers borne on erect stems 45—90 cm tall.

VI—X; ○ — ♃
10—40 cm;
taproot.
Stems: Prostrate to ascending.
Leaves: Alternate with roundish, palmately lobed blades.
Flowers:
2 — 4 in small axillary clusters, with a 3 lobed epicalyx and pink to white, darker veined, petals.
Fruits: 13—15 smooth, round nutlets, arranged in a ring.
Native to the eastern Mediterranean and Asia Minor; introduced long ago and now almost cosm.

1 — flower,
2 — fruit

2   1

Meadow Cranesbill

Geranium pratense L.

The geranium
or cranesbill
family
Geraniaceae

Meadow cranesbill is one of the loveliest of wild plants with its abundantly borne pale-violet-blue, saucer-shaped flowers. The ripe fruits have an interesting mode of seed dispersal; and, during dry and warm weather, it is possible to witness the sudden movement. The ripe fruits form beaks, which split into 5 parts, each of which curls sharply back catapulting the seeds about 2 metres.

The meadow cranesbill grows in meadows, ditches, and on river banks, mainly in lowlands and hilly regions, but only rarely in mountainous areas, where it is usually replaced by its relative, the wood cranesbill (*Geranium sylvaticum* L.), which has slightly darker and smaller flowers. Meadow cranesbill is often cultivated in gardens, along with its double-flowered, pink, white and striped forms.

VI—IX; ♃;
30—60 cm.
Rhizome: Stout.
Stems: Erect,
branched.
Leaves:
Petiolate,
palmate,
deeply lobed
with narrow
secondary lobes.
Flowers: Light
violet-blue,
nodding when
fading, erect
when fruit is
ripe.
Fruits: Beaked,
glandular-pilose.
Eu., As.;
naturalized in
N. Am.

1 — beaked fruit
after seeds have
been ejected

1

Common Cow-wheat

Melampyrum pratense L.

The anthirrhinum
or figwort family
Scrophulariaceae

As its Latin name suggests, the common cow-wheat grows in fields, but only in fields in the vicinity of woodland margins. Otherwise, it is a typical plant of light woods and thickets, being most common in oak forests, and also beech, spruce and pine woods with bilberries and heathers. Like all other cow-wheats it grows as a semi-parasite; it forms small disks on the roots where they touch neighbouring grass roots or other plants. From these disks vascular tissues unite with those of the host plant. It has no root hairs and takes in water with salts dissolved in it from other plants. It contains chlorophyll, and so the process of photosynthetic assimilation is normal.

The seeds have a small, oily swelling and attract ants, which are the chief agents of its distribution. The seeds contain a poisonous glycoside with narcotic effects; so the milk of cows, which graze in wood clearings with a large amount of the common cow-wheat, has an unpleasant taste. It is variable in appearance and can be mistaken for the wood cow-wheat (*M. sylvaticum* L.), from which it differs by a shorter and deep yellow corolla, as well as in other small features.

VI—VIII; ⊙;
10—50 cm.
Stem: Erect, with spreading branches.
Leaves: Opposite, lanceolate, sessile, entire.
Flowers: In axils of bracts in terminal raceme.
Calyx: With linear lobes.
Corolla: Two-lipped, whitish or lemon yellow.
Fruit: A capsule.
Eu., W. As.

1 — flower

1

Rough Hawkbit
Leontodon hispidus L.

Rough hawkbit blooms during the summer months in lawns, meadows and pastures, by roadsides and on stony slopes. It is plentiful in lowland and highland regions. One plant produces from several hundred to 2,000 haired achenes, which are readily borne away by the wind. It is interesting to observe this plant in its natural setting, as its flowers open early in the morning on sunny days, as early as 5 a. m., and close in the afternoon at about 3 p. m.

Rough hawkbit is fairly variable, and can often be seen in one habitat in both its hairy and smooth forms, which are sometimes divided into two varieties, or even into individual species. The autumnal hawkbit (*Leontodon autumnalis* L.) with its branched stems, more numerous, and smaller flower heads can be seen in similar places.

VI—X; ⚇;
15—30 cm.
Rhizome: Short.
Leaves: In basal rosette, oblanceolate, hairy or glabrous, entire or lobed.
Inflorescence: Erect flowering stem terminates in solitary head.
Flowers: Golden yellow, the outer florets sometimes reddish.
Achenes: Light brown, beaked, hairy. Eu., As.

Harebell (**Bluebell** in Scotland)

Campanula rotundifolia L.

The bellflower
family
Campanulaceae

The Latin name of this species, which produces a white, milky sap, is derived from the shape of its basal leaves, which are somewhat rounded in outline. It is a variable species, consisting of a number of varieties and forms. It can sometimes be found with white flowers. It grows most often on rocks, in pastures and dry woodland meadows, on banks, and at the edges of forests, in light pine woods and sometimes on walls. The nodding capsules contain a large number of small seeds, which are shaken out by the wind through three basal pores. These pores only open in dry weather. A strong wind can flick the seeds several metres away from the mother plant.

The anthers are the first to ripen in the flower, and the pollen clings to the surface of the yet unripe stigma. The stigmatic lobes unfold later and, if they have not been pollinated by insects, they can self-pollinate by curving back and contacting the pollen on the outer side of the style.

VI—IX; ♃;
10—30 cm.
Stems: Tufted,
sparingly
branched,
decumbent.
Leaves: Basal
petiolate,
rounded ovate,
cordate, upper
linear, entire.
Flowers: 1—2 cm
long, bell-shaped,
violet-blue.
Capsules:
Nodding
when ripe.
Eu., Siberia,
N. Am.

1 — capsule

1

Common St John's Wort

Hypericum perforatum L.

In summer, this plant covers sunny, grassy slopes, banks, dry meadows and woodland clearings with golden flowers. Its name is a reminder of the superstitions about the magic power of this plant, which, on St John's day, the 24th June, is in full blossom. Its flowers are yellow, but, when rubbed, the crushed cells release colouring matter, called hypericin, which turns red in the air. In the past, stories about its bewitching and magical powers became prevalent, because, when a cow had eaten a large quantity of the plant, its milk turned pinkish. This flower is not harmful to cattle, but other domestic animals, particularly sheep, are said to suffer inflammation of the skin if large quantities are consumed, especially in places unprotected by wool. It has a reputed medicinal value in illnesses of the digestive tract, kidneys and liver, while its oil extract soothes burns.

VI—VII; ♃;
30—70 cm.
Rhizome:
Branched.
Stems: Erect,
slightly
branched,
rounded, with
2 longitudinal
raised lines.
Leaves: Opposite,
ovate, entire,
with translucent
dots.
Flowers: In
a branched
inflorescence,
golden yellow
with a few black
dots.
Capsules: 8 mm
long, conical.
Eu., A., As.,
N. Af.;
introduced in
other parts of
the world.

1 — part of the
stem,
2 — capsule

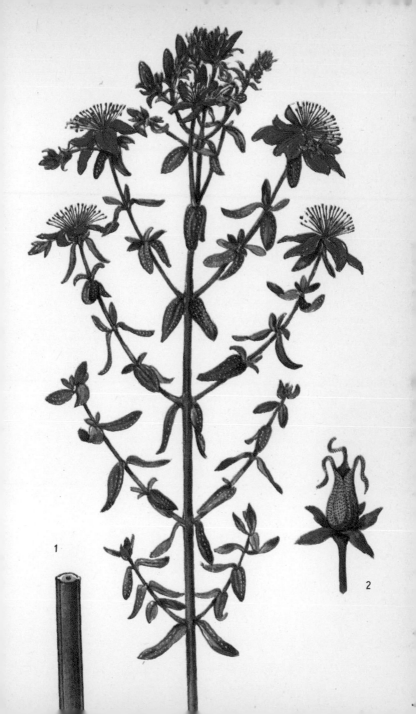

1

2

Creeping Thistle

Cirsium arvense (L.) SCOP.

The daisy family
Compositae

To the creeping thistle we owe the attractive globes of thistle down that ride the summer air. In all other respects however, it is one of the most troublesome weeds in fields and gardens. It can spread from uncultivated ground, from waste heaps, roadsides and stony slopes. Its extensively branching roots make it a tenacious weed. When the roots are cut or broken during digging or ploughing, every small piece starts growing from the root buds, and, in 2 to 3 years, one parent plant can form whole colonies. However, man, in his struggle against this weed, is helped by the natural occurence of virus infections, rust fungi, insect parasites and, last but not least, by partial dioecism, which limits the formation of seeds. An attempt has been made to infect colonies of the creeping thistle artificially with rust (*Puccinia suaveolens* [Pers.] Rostr.). Much more effective are some of the modern herbicides providing they are correctly used. A redeeming feature, however, is that the young plants provide good fodder for cattle, horses and pigs.

VI—IX; ⚃;
50—120 cm.
Rhizome:
Creeping.
Stems: Erect,
branching at the
top.
Leaves: Pinnatifid,
the lobes
ending in spines.
Flower heads:
1.5—2.5 cm in
diameter.
Florets:
Pale purple.
Achenes: 4 mm
long with long
pappus hairs
forming an
efficient
parachute.
Eu., As., N. Af.;
introduced in
N. Am.

Rosebay Willow-herb or Fireweed

Chamaenerion angustifolium (L.) SCOP.
(Syn. *Epilobium angustifolium* L.)

The fuchsia and willow-herb family
Onagraceae

The rosebay willow-herb spreads quickly through woodland clearings where large areas of trees have been killed by fire, or uprooted by gales. Where does it come from? The explanation is simple, as its tiny light seeds with a plume-like parachute of white hairs are easily carried by wind over large distances. These seeds are produced in large quantities, about 20,000 from each plant.

Fortunately, this plant is not a total weed, although its potential is not commonly known. Its flowers provide an abundance of nectar and pollen for bees. An area of 1 hectare, overgrown with this plant, can produce up to 500 kg of honey, or even more. The honey is light and greenish in colour, with a delicate and very sweet taste. Young, fresh leaves can be used as a salad vegetable, and have a high content of vitamin C, while the mature, dried ones contain tannin, and have been used as a substitute for tea. Its leaves are also reputed to have the ability to cure various inflammations. The sweet, underground rootstocks can be used as a vegetable, or for flour-making, and in some countries they were used in the preparation of an alcoholic drink; such domestic production may survive in some places even today.

VI—VIII; ♃;
60—140 cm.
Rhizome: Far creeping.
Stem: Erect, unbranched.
Leaves: Alternate, lanceolate, narrow, undersides veined.
Flowers: Dense terminal inflorescence, 4 sepals reddish on the outside, 4 petals rose-purple, sometimes white.
Capsules: Linear, shortly pubescent.
Eu., As., N. Am.

1 — capsule

1

Great Hairy Willow-herb or Codlins and Cream

Epilobium hirsutum L.

The fuchsia and willow-herb family
Onagraceae

The great hairy willow-herb often forms colonies in some regions along the banks of rivers, streams, canals and ponds, or in roadside ditches in lowland and highland areas. It prefers calcareous soils, and is one of those plants with flowers that produce a large quantity of nectar. The content of vitamin C in its leaves is relatively high, about 140 mg in 100 g of vegetation.

In Ancient Greece a herb called *oinotheras* assumed an important place in legends, as its roots were said to have the power to tame any wild animal. Botanists believe that this plant was the great hairy willow-herb.

There are many species of willow-herb growing in Europe and elsewhere. Individual species may hybridize naturally and so it is possible to find plants difficult to name. Several of the dwarfer, larger flowered species are grown in gardens.

VI—IX; 2↓;
60—150 cm.
Underground stolons: Stout, fleshy and far creeping.
Stem: Erect, branched, rounded, with spreading hairs.
Leaves: Sessile, oblong-lanceolate, serrate.
Flowers: Up to 2 cm long, rose-pink.
Stigma: With 4 lobes.
Seeds: With short pappus.
Eu., As.

1 — capsule

1

Knotgrass

Polygonum aviculare L.

The knotgrass is one of the most variable species of plants, with a number of varieties, subspecies, several of which are sometimes treated as separate species. It can grow in abundance in fairly frequented places, by roads, in playgrounds and yards, on paths, between paving stones, on rubbish heaps, and as a weed in fields.

The northern or boreal knotgrass (*Polygonum boreale* [Large] Small), is much more robust, with oblong to obovate leaves. It is restricted to northernmost Europe — Iceland, Greenland, Shetland, northern Scandinavia and eastern Canada.

Its seeds are sometimes used as bird food. A high content of silicic acid has resulted in the knotgrass, like other plants containing this acid, being used in the treatment of tuberculosis. It may still be used for curing certain internal illnesses, and for reducing inflammation of the chest.

It has been found that when large quantities of this plant are eaten by white or piebald animals it can cause inflammation of the skin when associated with hot sunsine. The common St John's wort (*Hypericum perforatum* L.*) also causes a similar reaction.

VI—XI; ⊙;
10—100 cm.
Stems: Slender, wiry, prostrate, branching.
Leaves: Elliptic, lanceolate or linear, up to 3 cm or more long.
Flowers: Solitary or 2—5 in leaf axils, whitish, greenish or pinkish, 2—3 mm long.
Fruit: A triangular nutlet 1.5—4.5 mm. Today almost cosm.

1 — flower

1

Purple Loosestrife

Lythrum salicaria L.

The loosestrife
and crape-myrtle
family
Lythraceae

The slender, rosy-purple flower spikes of the purple loosestrife in summer decorate the banks of rivers, streams and ponds, damp meadows and ditches. Its tiny, sticky seeds are easily spread by the feet and feathers of water birds, often over long distances. This is the reason why this plant has spread to so many parts of the temperate world.

The structure of its flowers is interesting. They appear in three forms: 1. a short style and a mixture of long and medium length stamens; 2. a medium style and long and short stamens; 3. a long style with short and medium length stamens. Each stamen-type also produces pollen grains of a distinct size. These variations greatly aid cross-pollination. The flowers contain nectar and are visited by bees. Several improved selections of purple loosestrife are grown in gardens, varying from pink and white to rich purple.

Infusions made from its rootstocks and stems were used to stop diarrhoea and the fresh leaves when crushed are said to slow down local bleeding. The young shoots and leaves were used as a vegetable, while the red dye from its flowers has been used in confectionery. The rootstocks contain tannin and are used by the fishermen of the Caspian and Black Sea regions for preserving fishing nets and other equipment to prevent rotting in sea water.

VI—IX; ♃;
50—120 cm.
Stem: Erect, woody at the base, branched, square in cross section.
Leaves: Lanceolate, sessile, up to 12 cm long.
Inflorescence: Dense, spike-like.
Flowers: Rose-purple.
Sepals: 6 with 6 longer teeth in between.
Petals: 6 obovate.
Capsule: Oblong. 3—4 mm long, enclosed in the calyx.
Eu., As., N. Af.; elsewhere introduced.

1 — flower

152

1

Common Mullein or Aaron's Rod

Verbascum thapsus L.

The antirrhinum
or figwort family
Scrophulariaceae

The tall, robust common mullein, with its yellow flowers, grows on well-drained, sunny slopes and gravelly river banks, in pastures, quarries and woodland clearings. The plant is adapted to dry conditions, as it is densely clothed in whitish hairs, which protect it from excessive dehydration and overheating. Its broad upper leaves, which narrow to their junction with the stem, direct the rain water straight to the roots, so that the plant may take full advantage of it, while the basal rosette of flat leaves shades the soil surrounding the plant.

The common mullein is sometimes mistaken for the large-flowered mullein (*V. thapsiforme* Schrad.), used for medicinal purposes. It can be distinguished from this, its closest relative, by its smaller size, by its cupped flowers, which are only 1.5—3 cm wide, and also by the long-hairy filaments of its glabrous stamens, which are 4 times longer than the anthers. The large-flowered mullein, on the other hand, has flat flowers, 3—5 cm wide, and filaments only twice as long as the anthers. The common mullein also has a distinct smell, which reputedly repels mice. Its poisonous seeds have been used to drug fish.

VII—IX; ☉;
30—200 cm.
Stem: Erect, usually unbranched.
Leaves: Alternate, obovate-lanceolate, decurrent on the stem, crenate, stem and leaves with soft whitish wool.
Flowers:
About 1.5—3 cm in diameter, pale yellow.
Fruit:
An ovoid capsule.
Eu., W. As.

1 — flower

1

Fat Hen
Chenopodium album L.

The fat hen can be a troublesome weed in fields and gardens, especially amongst root crops and vegetables. It also grows in large numbers on rubbish heaps, on fallow land, along roads and on manure and compost heaps. It produces considerable quantities of seeds, which can number as many as a hundred thousand on a single well-grown plant. Individual seeds on one plant can vary in size and colour, from black and brown to pale yellow. Their ability to germinate also differs, as, generally speaking, light seeds germinate earlier and quicker than dark ones. To develop large plants, fat hen requires a moist, fertile soil, but it is tolerant and can grow almost anywhere. It can also have an adverse effect on some plants, especially sugar beet, to which it is related as it harbours various mutual diseases.

It has been growing in cultivated soils ever since the early Stone Age as a weed, but served a useful purpose also, as its seeds were used as a grain substitute. Today, whole plants may be used in the preparation of silage. The leaves can be used as a substitute for spinach.

VII—X; ⊙;
10—100 cm or more.
Stem: Erect, usually branched.
Leaves: Ovate-lanceolate, irregularly toothed, upper narrower, almost entire.
Flowers: Tiny, greenish, densely clustered and arranged in a leafy panicle; with 5 petals, 5 stamens and a pistil with a bifid stigma.
Ripe seeds: Almost smooth, shiny black.
Today almost cosm.

1 — fruiting cluster

1

Water-pepper

Polygonum hydropiper L.

The rhubarb and dock family
Polygonaceae

The water-pepper is appropriately named. The plant has a burning, bitter taste, which serves as a warning to cattle. If eaten in large quantitites in hot sunshine, it can cause dangerous inflammation of the skin, just as the common St. John's wort (*Hypericum perforatum* L.*). It irritates sensitive skin when touched by people allergic to it. Blistering can also be caused if contact is maintained through constant handling. Its chemical composition has not yet been fully analysed. It contains glycosides, which cause blood clotting, tannin, some organic acids and other substances. It was widely used for medicinal purposes.

It grows in colonies in damp or muddy soil on the banks of rivers and ponds, on damp paths through woods, in ditches, in damp fields and on the empty beds of ponds; sometimes also in shallow water.

VII—X; ⊙;
20—70 cm.
Stem: Erect or ascending, usually sparingly branched.
Leaves:
Lanceolate, slender pointed.
Inflorescence.
Interrupted, leafy in lower part, nodding above.
Flowers: Greenish, rarely pinkish, (3—) 4 segments, externally covered with yellow glandular dots.
Fruit: Ovoid to triangular, 2.5—3.5 mm long, dark brown or black.
Eu., As.

1 — flower

1

Corn Mint

Mentha arvensis L.

The dead-nettle
and mint family
Labiatae

This aromatic perennial grows abundantly as a weed in damp fields, on fallow land, marshy meadows and pastures, in ditches and thickets, and on river banks. It contains silicic acid, as do all mints, the most important component of which is menthol. Menthol, even when diluted, can destroy certain bacteria. Corn mint is used for preparing herbal teas and syrups, in confectionery and cosmetics, as an ingredient in toothpastes and mouth washes, and in liqueurs. For such purposes, the extract is taken from cultivated species of the peppermint (*M.* × *piperita* L.) and from the spearmint (*M. spicata* L.), as the wild types only contain a low percentage of menthol. A dressing made from the fresh leaves of corn mint, when placed on the forehead, is soothing for headaches.

It is a variable plant, easily hybridizing with other species. It propagates by seed and spreads by underground stolons.

VII—IX; ♃;
5—25 cm.
Underground stolons: Creeping.
Stems: Both prostrate and ascending, square in cross section, branched.
Leaves: Opposite, ovate, serrate.
Flowers: Clustered whorls in axils of upper leaves, purple.
Calyx: Bell-shaped.
Corolla: With a short tube.
Stames: 4.
Achenes: 4.
Eu., As., N. Am.

1 — flower

1

Bracken

Pteridium aquilinum (L.) KUHN

The bracken
family
Dennstaedtiaceae

The common bracken fern often forms a continuous cover in dry woods, especially pine forests, and in oak forests on acid soils. It also grows in woodland clearings, or among heather on moorland. It thrives in humus-rich, sandy, moist — but not wet — and rather acidic soils; rarely on limy soils. It needs plenty of light but will tolerate semi-shade. Bracken is the tallest native European fern. A slanting cut through the base of the stem reveals a pattern of tissues that is reminiscent of a two-headed eagle.

It is considered a useful fern in woods, as it shelters the soil, and its rootstocks improve the soil structure; although sometimes it can prevent the natural regeneration of trees from seeds. In places where bracken grows profusely the dried foliage is used as a litter for farm stock.

VII—X; 2↓;
20—200 cm
or more.
Rhizome:
Branched.
Leaves: Solitary,
long-stalked, with
triangular blades,
3—4 times
pinnate, tough.
Spore-bearing sori:
Under the curved
margins of leaf
segments.
Cosm. with
several distinct
forms or
subspecies.

1 — leaf segment,
2 — segments
with marginal
sori

Common Polypody

Polypodium vulgare L.

The polypody
family
Polypodiaceae

The common polypody fern has deeply pinnatifid leaves which remain green in winter. It grows on shady rocks, stony slopes or in mossy and stony woodland soil, and sometimes even as an epiphyte on the mossy branches and trunks of trees. It requires semi-or full shade, and moist conditions.

The rootstock initially has a sweet taste, but on chewing it soon becomes bitter. It has been used for medicinal purposes for a long time, although its properties have not been analysed in detail. It has been used against intestinal worms, and as a cure for coughs and bronchitis.

Common polypody varies considerably, especially in the shape of its leaves, and the structure of its sori. Indeed, the two most distinctive variants are now usually given separate specific rank. Sometimes, abnormally large leaves can be found and forms occur with forked or crested segments. Such forms are sometimes cultivated.

VIII—IX; $2\!\!\downarrow$;
10—40 cm.
Rhizome:
Branched,
creeping, covered
with brown
scales.
Leaves: Petiolate,
tough, pinnatifid,
glabrous.
Sori: Orbicular,
without scales
on the underside
of leaves, in
rows about
midway between
midrib and leaf
margins.
Eu., As., N. Am.,
N. Af.

Heather or Ling

Calluna vulgaris (L.) HULL

The heather
family
Ericaceae

To some people the flowering of heather announ-ces the end of the summer holidays, though its flowering season lasts from the end of July until October. It grows in pine and oak forests on acid soils, in old peat bogs and on moorlands. In northern Germany and in England it spreads over vast areas, growing in acid soils, poor in minerals, and is generally indicative of thin infertile soils. Heather thrives in damp cool con-ditions, particularly in maritime climates. It does not tolerate intense winter cold and can suffer during prolonged drought. Its roots live in association with certain species of fungi, without which it is unable to function. Heather is a most variable plant and hundreds of different forms are known and cultivated in gardens. Some are completely prostrate in habit, others form compact bun-like hummocks; others are densely white hairy or have double flowers. Flower colour ran-ges from white, through a range of pinks, to rich purple.

Heather flowers provide bees with an abundan-ce of nectar at the end of summer, but the honey is dark, and does not appeal to all people. The foliage has been used in herbal preparations for the treatment of rheumatic fever, and kidney and bladder inflammations. A tea prepared from its dried flowers and stems is liked by some people.

VIII—X; shrub; 5—60 cm.
Branches: Erect or ascending.
Leaves:
Linear, opposite, overlapping.
Calyx and corolla:
Pale purple or white; small corolla hidden within the calyx.
Fruit: A globose capsule 2—2.5 mm long.
Eu., Asia Minor, W. Siberia; introduced in N. Am.

1 — detail of a branch with linear leaves and flowers

1

THE HERBARIUM, A PERMANENT RECORD

As long as 450 years ago an Italian, Luca Ghini, (d. 1556) recommended drying and pressing as the best method of plant preservation. This was the beginning of the first herbarium, or collection of preserved plants, which soon became the accepted mode for botanists: The oldest preserved herbarium is kept in Rome; its creator was the botanist, Gherardo Cibo, a pupil of Luca Ghini, and he made it in 1532. Thanks to this method, the Swedish naturalist, Carl von Linné (Linnaeus, 1707—1778), was able to describe and classify all plants known at that time on the basis of thousands of herbarium specimens collected from all over the world. Even today, the herbarium has not lost its importance, and still remains an irreplaceable botanical aid.

The world's collections contain hundreds of millions of herbarium specimens, which are used for the purpose of daily scientific research. In addition, the herbarium is of considerable aid to the amateur botanist. It teaches him to recognize the distinctive features of individual species and enables him to make comparisons, and refresh his knowledge at any time of the year. Anybody can start a general collection of plants growing wild in his area, or make a specific survey of field and garden weeds, or catalogue herbs. There are many instances of people who started to collect plants as a hobby, then became so deeply involved in the subject that they were eventually recognized as experts on flora, and as having contributed greatly to botanical knowledge. But where should one start?

First, one should become acquainted with the flora of the neighbourhood by taking regular walks to different places from spring through to autumn. After this the collection of plant specimens can begin. The basic equipment needed for such field trips would include a map for pinpointing accurately the habitats of flora, a notebook and pencil, a hand-lens with a magnification power of × 10 or higher, a fern trowel made of good steel and measuring 25 cm by 4 cm, a pocket knife, and, finally, a bundle of small packets for seeds. Plant specimens should be put in large plastic bags, which should then, preferably, be put in a linen bag which can be slung over the shoulder. If one is going to collect a large number of specimens, the full plastic bag can be conveniently placed in a rucksack, and the linen bag refilled with empty ones.

Several sheets of drying paper in a case may be included in the equipment, if plants are to be pressed on the spot. Sheets of newsprint may be adequate for the initial pressing, and the specimen should be identified by a label with the name of the locality and the date, to guard against any errors of memory. Some plants must be pressed directly on the spot, as their leaves soon wither, and their flowers droop. Then the plant is useless. Delicate, aquatic plants, the annual speedwells *(Veronica)*, poppy *(Papaver*)* and anemone *(Anemone*)* are good examples of such flowers.

A reference book, a camera, a compass, and a metal hook or grapple, on a nylon string, for reaching water plants, might also prove useful on such field trips.

It is best to avoid collecting specimens during wet weather or when they are covered by early morning dew, because wet plants take a long time to dry out, and can easily mould and rot. In contrast, other plants must be dampened deliberately. Thick roots, which contain too much soil, can be washed in a stream, and quickly dried in the air; then the plant can be safely stored in the plastic bag.

Some system of recording features of the terrain and plant life while collecting is very important. Entries in the notebook should consist of an accurate map reference of the locality, and a detailed description of the topography and of all the discovered plants, with notes about their frequency. The specimen taken for the herbarium should be accompanied by further notes about the colour of the flowers, which can change with drying, about the sheen of the leaves etc. Each locality must be numbered separately.

Different plants demand different methods of collection.

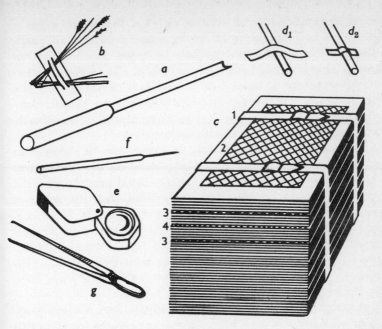

Fig. 7. Equipment for the collection and preparation of plants: a — fern trowel, b — the use of a slit strip paper to hold the bent stems of a plant during drying, c — plant press ready for use (1 — fastening straps, 2 — wooden frame with lattice centre, 3 — corrugated paper, 4 — plant is placed between two sheets of drying paper) d_1 — incorrect way to secure a dried plant, d_2 — correct way to secure a plant, e — hand-lens, f — dissecting needle, g — forceps.

Small species are always collected in larger quantity from a single locality. Tall plants are too big for the herbarium, so the top part with flowers or fruits is cut off, as well as the middle section with several leaves, and, finally, the bottom part. Beginners often make the mistake of collecting only the flowering top part of the plant for their herbarium, and discover later that certain important features essential for determination are missing, such as the roots, the stolons, the basal rosette of leaves, the sterile shoots, or the fruit. If the whole plant cannot be taken, then its most important part should be collected.

Long grasses should never be cut, but bent instead several times in the shape of the letters V, N or M according to the size of the herbarium sheets. The bent sections are then covered with strips of paper to prevent the stem breaking.

The collected specimens should be put between the pressing sheets as soon as possible after the excursion, if this has not been done already in the field. The plant is arranged on the paper, so that some leaves are turned with their right side, and others with the underside upwards. A label, with data about the locality and the possible preliminary classification of the plant, should be attached. When a large number of specimens is collected, and it is impossible to produce detailed labels at the same time, it is sufficient to enter the number of the locality as recorded in the notebook and the date of collection. The individual double sheets of pressing paper, with the plants between them, are then stored with similar size pieces of corrugated cardboard around them to enable the air to circulate. A pile of them, 30—35 cm thick at the most is then placed in a plant press. An easily made press consists of two pieces of plywood, or wire netting stretched over a wooden or metal frame. Finally everything is secured by straps and placed in a warm and dry place, even close to a stove. If collections of plants for the herbarium are being made continuously, then a metal pedestal with a metal base and sides and a grating at the top, with a heater (a small two-plate electric cooker is sufficient) installed at the bottom, is very useful. The presses are then put on the grating, so that the open ends of the cardboard face the source of heat. In the latest drying methods, infra-red radiators are often used. Plants can also be dried without a heater, by covering each pile with weights. During the first few days, the plants should be transferred, at least once a day, to dry sheets, and the leaves and flowers rearranged again during the first change of paper. After 4 or 5 days, it is sufficient to change the sheets every other day.

When the leaves and stems remain rigid on the plant being lifted, it means that the plant has already dried out. The stage of dampness inside the press can be, initially, tested with the fingers. Plants must not be dried too much, as they would break and crumble; not all plants take the same length of time to dry out. For example grasses *(Gramineae)*, members of the *Cyperaceae* family and slender plants dry very quickly, while fleshy plants retain their moisture for a long time. Plants from both categories should not, if at all possible, be placed in the same press. In certain cases, some plants require special treatment before drying. Fleshy plants, such as the stonecrops *(Sedum*)*, the houseleeks *(Sempervivum)* and others, which would continue growing in the herbarium for a long time, with the ensuing deformation of their stems as a result of the lack of light, are submersed for 30 seconds to 2 minutes in boiling water. Similarly, special preparations are also carried out for bulbs, rootstocks and tubers of some other plants. These fleshy, subterranean organs are cut lengthwise into two or more segments, before they are plunged into boiling water. Afterwards, several layers of paper are used for drying out such fleshy plants.

After several weeks, the dry plants are taken out from the drying sheets and arranged on their final paper. The best paper for the herbarium is white, or light grey, or yellow wrapping paper, cut into sheets of an approximate size 42×29.5 cms (or 42×28 cms, 44×27 cms, or 44×29 cms, the last being the size used internationally). The plants are neatly spread out on the sheet and stuck to it by thin strips of linen tape (selotape can be used but deteriorates over the years and turns yellow), while a space is left for the label in the right-hand corner at the bottom of the sheet. Plants should never be smeared with glue along their entire length, nor should they be sown on by cotton, as it may be necessary to remove them for study. Finally the loose, ripe fruits and seeds are put in small transparent packets, and the separate flower can be displayed and spread out in detail, if one has been prepared for this purpose before drying. Only specimens of a single species from a particular locality should be displayed on each sheet of paper.

The label is mounted in the right-hand corner at the bottom of the sheet. It is important to pay special attention to its presentation. It is best typed on a card measuring 12×8 cms (or 14×10 cms, or 10.5×7.5 cms) and it should contain the following data:

a) the name of the owner
b) the name of the region
c) the scientific name of the species
d) the vernacular name of the species
e) the locality (including map reference) and the habitat (including soil or rock types if possible and altitude)
f) the date of collection
g) the name of the collector
h) the name of the person who named or checked the naming of the collection

An example for a herbarium label:

Herbarium of Arthur Hook
Flora of Dumfries
Anemone nemorosa L.
Wood Anemone

Thornill: oak forest on the south-eastern slope of Queensberry (696 m); 2 km east of the village, ca 260 m above sea level; primary rocks slate.

28. 4. 1972   Collected by: A. Hook
Named by: G. Hill

The labels may be preprinted, with a schematic map of the region, in which case each collection should be marked in red.

The herbarium specimens of one genus, or, in larger herbaria, of one species, are placed in folders made from wrapping paper double the size of that used for the individual sheet of pressed plants. The name of the genus and species is entered in the left-hand corner at the bottom of it. Envelopes containing genera of one family are either tied up between hard covers, or stored in special boxes with a hinged or deep fitting lid, which can be constructed according to the size of the herbarium envelopes. Each collector can determine his own system of arranging his specimens, but it is best to classify them by follow-

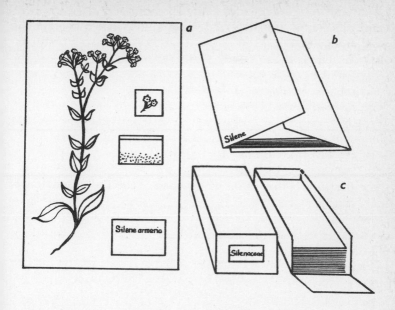

Fig. 8. Herbarium operations: a — example of herbarium sheet with mounted plant, dissected flower, envelope with ripe fruit or seeds, b — folder for 8—15 herbarium sheets, c — herbarium box with hinged front.

ing a standard flora of the region, or using the sequence of families devised by Engler or Bentham and Hooker. Herbarium folders must always be carried in a horizontal position, and the sheets should not be turned in the same way as the pages of a book; separate sheets must be handled without turning them over, so that the plants always face upwards. The large national herbaria use special cabinets designed for this purpose, with close-fitting doors to prevent dust, dampness and insects entering and damaging the dry plants. The herbarium must be carefully checked and looked after. Such care includes the disinfection of the specimens and the whole storage room at least once a year. Naphtalene, globol (paradichlorbensen) or toluen (Mirban oil) or a mixture of globol, toluen and methylated spirits may be permanently placed in the case. Museums, and other institutions with large herbarium collections, use the poisonous fumes of sulphide of carbon for disinfection. Special air-tight cases lined with zinc, with a lid slotting into a groove filled with glycerol solution are used for this purpose. The bottle containing sulphide of carbon is placed at the bottom of the case. Because the substance is inflammable and explosive, great care is required. Details of the process can be found in botanical literature.

The herbarium specimens can be named at any time, but the best time is usually winter. Besides the relevant flora, a general, or a specialists, monograph, depending on the material to be identified, a hand-lens, sharp forceps and two dissecting needles are needed. Before making a detailed study of the internal structure of a flower deformed during pressing, the flower must be gently boiled in a little water.

Finally, several points must be made about collecting plants in the field. It is a mistake to think that the herbarium should contain only rare plants. That could be very harmful both for conservation and botanical science. Rare plants are, in fact, often protected by law. The herbarium, therefore, should principally contain relatively common plants, or plants taken from places where the natural environment is being obliterated by, say, building construction.

CONCLUSION

First, it is important to get to know the natural environment of a particular country fully. The more people who penetrate its secrets, the more people will begin to understand nature; and the greater will be the chance of preserving the full beauty of nature for future generations. The countryside is in great danger at present. The narrow circle of specialized biologists cannot save it. So it is necessary to get people from all fields of human activity involved, especially those who can influence the issue favourably by their decisions. Ignorance and lack of interest about this could prove to be very harmful for mankind.

GLOSSARY

area — the surface occupied by a taxon (i.e. species, genus, family)

autotrophic organism — one capable of changing inorganic compounds into organic ones without external intervention (i.e. green plants, sulphureous bacteria)

chlorophyll — the green pigment located in chloroplasts, plastids occurring in cells of algae and higher plants

cuticle — a thin, waxen film on the surface of plants

ecology — science concerned with the interrelationship of organisms and their environments

ecosystem — a complex of organisms (plant and animal) and environment, forming in nature a functioning whole

edaphic — relating to the soil

endemics — taxa restricted or native to a particular area or region

etiolation — the loss of chlorophyll in a green plant caused by the lack of light, accompanied by excessively elongated growth

guttation — the secretion of surplus water in the form of drops through hydathodes, water-excreting glands on the edges and tips of leaves

habitat — a complex of climatic and soil factors effecting and interrelating with the vegetation in a given area

halophytes — plants growing in a salt-rich soil

heliophytes — plants growing in sunny places

helophytes — plants growing in wet or constantly moist soil

hydrophyte — an aquatic plant

isotherm — a line connecting points on the Earth's surface having the same temperature

locality — the geographically determined place of occurrence

macroclimate — a climate covering large areas of the Earth's surface

mesophytes — plants growing under average conditions of soil moisture and warmth (relative to a temperate climate)

microclimate — the climate of a limited habitat where some particular factor differentiates it from its surroundings (e.g. in a crown of a tree, in a ravine or in a pond)

osmotic pressure — the pressure under which a weak solution of dissolved salts penetrates through a semipermeable membrane into a concentrated solution

photosynthesis (photosynthetic assimilation) — the biological process during which a complex organic substance is formed from simple substances with the help of the sun's radiation

phytogeography — study of ranges of plants over the Earth and of the causes of their distribution

relicts — plants surviving today in places where they have endured long-term, adverse conditions (i.e. glacial relicts, tertiary relicts)

spore — the basic reproductive cell of primitive plants such as fungi, mosses and ferns

stomata — breathing pores in the epidermis of plants with two contracting cells

succulents — plants with fleshy stems or leaves that store considerable amounts of water

taxon — any basic unit of systematic classification (i.e. variety, subspecies, species, genus, family)

transpiration — water loss from plants into the atmosphere in the form of water vapour, mainly via the stomata

turgor — the internal pressure in a plant cell

xerophytes — plants found in dry places and adapted for life in such conditions

BIBLIOGRAPHY

Butcher R. W.: *A New Illustrated British Flora*. 2 vols. London, 1961.

Cain S. A. and G. M. de Oliveira Castro: *Manual of Vegetation Analysis*. New York, 1959.

Clapham A. R., T. G. Tutin and E. F. Warburg: *Flora of the British Isles*. 2nd Edition. Cambridge, 1962.

Clapham A. R., T. G. Tutin and E. F. Warburg: *Excursion Flora of the British Isles*. 2nd Edition. Cambridge, 1968.

Cronqüist A.: *The Evolution and Classification of Flowering Plants*. Boston, 1968.

Daubenmire R. F.: *Plants and Environment. A Textbook of Plant Autoecology*. New York, 1947.

Esau K.: *Plant Anatomy*. New York, 1953.

Hanson H.: *Dictionary of Ecology*. London, 1962.

Hutchinson J.: *Evolution and Phylogeny of Flowering Plants*. London and New York, 1969.

Kramer P. J.: *Plant and Soil Water Relationships*. New York, Toronto and London, 1949.

McClintock D. and Fitter R. S. R.: *The Pocket Guide to Wild Flowers*. London, 1956.

Oosting H. J.: *The Study of Plant Communities. An Introduction to Plant Ecology*. San Francisco, 1958.

Perring F. H. and S. M. Walters Ed.: *Atlas of the British Flora:* London, 1962.

Roles S. J.: *Illustrations for Flora of the British Isles by Clapham, Tutin and Warburg*. (4 vols). London, 1957—65.

Ross-Craig S.: *Drawings of British Plants*. London, 1951 to 1972 (published in separate parts at intervals).

Savile D. B. O.: *Collection and Care of Botanical Specimens*. Ottawa, 1962.

Sinnott E. W. and K. S. Wilson: *Botany: Principles and Problems*. 5th Edition. New York, London and Toronto, 1955.

Tansley A. G.: *Introduction to Plant Ecology*. London, 1946.

Tansley A. G. and E. P. Evans: *Plant Ecology and the School*. London.

Van Dyne G. M., Ed.: *The Ecosystem Concept in Natural Resource Management*. New York and London, 1969.

Walker D. and R. G. West, Ed.: *Studies in the Vegetational History of the British Isles*. London, 1970.

Weisz P. B. and M. S. Fuller: *The Science of Botany*. New York, San Francisco, Toronto and London, 1962.

INDEX OF COMMON NAMES

INDEX OF LATIN NAMES